An Introduction to
MACROECONOMICS

Second Edition

Gwen Eudey

PEARSON

Custom
Publishing

Printed in the United States of America

10 9 8 7 6 5 4 3 2 1

ISBN 0-536-32427-1

2006160651

JK

Please visit our web site at *www.pearsoncustom.com*

PEARSON CUSTOM PUBLISHING
75 Arlington Street, Suite 300, Boston, MA 02116
A Pearson Education Company

CONTENTS

AN INTRODUCTION TO MACROECONOMICS

1.1 INTRODUCTION

Macroeconomic modeling extends the study of microeconomics that you began in your introductory coursework. We will build on many of the tools and concepts you learned in your introductory micro class: we will use graphs to determine market equilibria, we'll make assumptions about which markets function perfectly competitively and which do not, and we'll even model some of the same markets that you did in micro.

What makes macroeconomics different from micro, is that while microeconomics studies markets for particular goods or services in isolation from each other, macroeconomics is the study not only of each of those markets but also how each of those markets interact with each other. Macroeconomics is the study of the whole economy at once.

1.2 MACROECONOMICS: AN EXTENSION OF MICROECONOMIC THEORY

Consider two economic models you may have seen in your Introductory Microeconomics course:

1. Households have utility for goods, which determines the amount they are willing to pay at any quantity; those goods in turn cost something to produce, which determines the sale price of goods at any quantity. Equilibrium exists where, at some quantity traded, the price households are willing to pay is equal to the minimum amount a firm will charge for that quantity.

2. Individuals supply labor in order to earn a wage, but they also value their leisure time; Firms want to hire workers but also want to maximize their profits so they are only willing to pay workers as much as the value of their production. Equilibrium exists where, at some quantity of labor traded, the wage firms are willing to pay exactly compensates workers for the utility value of the leisure time they've given up.

To a *microeconomist*, the labor and goods markets may be studied in isolation and in great detail. To a *macroeconomist*, these two markets are linked in important ways. Households make consumption and labor decision that impact and interact with firms' employment and production choices. Firms employ workers from many different households, and households may or may not consume the goods produced at firms to which they lend money or at which they work. In other words, every agent in the economy depends in some way on every other agent in the economy, and so macroeconomics is the study of all markets in the economy at once.

Macroeconomics uses the theories from micro to understand choices within each market, and also attempts to understand the linkages between those markets; this is illustrated in the stylized example in **Figure 1**.

Figure 1 depicts an economy in which there are three households and three firms. Each household supplies labor to one firm, and each firms sells output to one different household. If Household 2, for example, were to increase its demand for goods, then Firm 2 would demand more labor from Household 1, which would impact Household 1 spending on good 1, which would affect the demand by Firm 1 for labor from Household 3 and so on.

In the real world, different households consume things from many firms, and firms also purchase supplies (inputs) from other firms; those complications however only serve to make the linkages between people in the economy even stronger than those in the simple example in **Figure 1**. Because the behavior of every household is linked to that of every other firm and

FIGURE 1: ILLUSTRATION OF THE INTERACTION OF MARKETS IN THE MACRO-ECONOMY

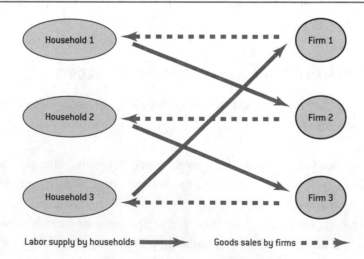

household in the economy, something that affects a market for one particular good will affect labor and consumption decisions throughout the macro-economy.

1.3 THE MACROECONOMIC MODEL

A macroeconomic model would ideally distinguish between the markets for red apples and green apples within the grouping of consumer goods, between skilled and unskilled workers within the category employment, and so on. There could, in principle, be as many markets in the macroeconomic model as there are workers and households and firms, because each one is in some way different from every other! A model with so many markets would be very difficult to work with, however, and so the goal of the macroeconomist is to make the model as simple as possible without losing vital information about how the economy works.

In microeconomics, you became comfortable with looking at supply curves for a firm and then also considering the supply curve for the industry as a whole; behind that industry supply curve lay an *industry-wide production function* that represented the combined hiring and capital investment decisions of many different firms. The assumption was not that every firm was the same size as every other one, but that each firm would behave in the same way if they were faced with the same choices.

In macroeconomics, we group many industries together into what is called an *Aggregate Production Function*. The industries produce different goods, have different costs, and are of varying sizes, and there is further variation across firms within industries. The underlying assumption is that because these industries are so closely linked to each other, production in each industry will tend to rise and fall at the same time, and so the modeling assumption is that we can treat all the industries in the aggregate in the same way and just look at one aggregate market.

Figure 2 plots the quantity of production in several different aggregations, or groupings, of U.S. industries over the period 1977-2001; each series is scaled so that the level in 1996 is equal

FIGURE 2: PRODUCTION QUANTITY INDEXES (scaling sets 1996 = 100 for each series)

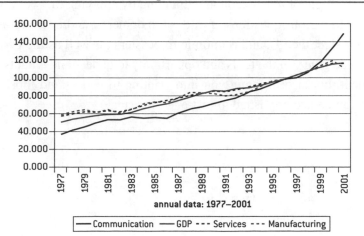

annual data: 1977–2001

— Communication —— GDP --- Services --- Manufacturing

to 100 (that makes it easier to compare across the series). One aggregation in the figure is a measure of the production of *all* goods and services—known as *Gross Domestic Product* (GDP). GDP corresponds to the output of the Aggregate Production Function we'll use in our macro-economic model.

As can be seen in **Figure 2**, movements in GDP are representative of movements in many industrial groupings: Production in the communications industry, for example, grew much more quickly in the 1990s than it did in other industries. Consequently, a model that uses GDP to represent all production in the economy will miss some important aspects of the economy. On the other hand, because a great deal is gained in terms of the simplicity of a model that treats all goods as going into one market, that is the model we will use throughout the course. We will find that even this model is rather complicated, and remains rich enough to teach us much about how the macro-economy works.

As you might expect, there are significantly more complicated macroeconomic models of the economy than the one we'll use in this introductory course! As we go along, we'll discuss things we observe in the real-world data that are areas of exploration in more advanced macroeconomic models. Models that are primarily concerned with issues of income distribution, variations in labor market power across skill groups, the impact of racial, gender, or other prejudices on employment opportunities, and many other exciting topics, all fall within the realm of macro-economics but outside the realm of the introductory course! You will see, however, that there is a great deal that we can learn from the standard introductory model of the economy we will study in this text.

1.4 WHAT TO DO WITH A MACROECONOMIC MODEL

Economics has its roots in philosophy: The intricacies and subtleties of an abstract economic model of human and market interactions have a deep basis in logic; that logical underpinning would be, for many, enough to make economics interesting even if there were no practical applications!

Macroeconomic modeling however is not restricted to philosophers and academics, but is used (and misused!) by policymakers, development workers, stock brokers, businesses, the myriad of economic consulting firms that are hired by those groups, and others. In this text you will be taught the logic of macroeconomic thinking by applying the workhorse model used throughout the text to various questions of interest to domestic and international policymakers (and the people who elect them!), and economic forecasters (as well as the people who hire them!). The objective is to give you the tools and opportunity to understand what is going on in the economic environment, but also to tempt you into wanting to understand those things in a much deeper way than can be accomplished in just one semester.

MACROECONOMIC DATA: OUTPUT AND PRICE AGGREGATES

2.1 INTRODUCTION

In macroeconomics, as in microeconomics, we will be looking at models in which prices and quantities adjust in response to changes in supply and demand. Because the model simultaneously considers motivations by households and firms, we simplify things by assuming there is one production function that represents production of all goods and services in the economy. While that is a simplifying modeling assumption, it requires that if we want to apply the model to real-world data, we will need real-world data to be aggregated (combined) in the same way that it is in the model.

How can we measure the sum of all production of apples, oranges, computers, rolled steel, legal services, etc to get "Aggregate Gross Domestic Product"—the measure of Quantity in our macro model? How can we calculate one single "price" that represents the intersection of Supply and Demand for all of those goods and services? The answer is that we construct economic *indexes* of quantities and prices.

2.2 CREATING ECONOMIC AGGREGATES: THE INDEX

Consider the old question of how one might go about adding apples and oranges. One could measure them in bushels, pounds, or value, but in any of those cases, the idea is to group unlike objects (apples and oranges) by "weighting" each one by some value (bushels, pounds, or dollars). The outcome is what is called a *quantity index*—where the quantities are "indexed" or weighted by their contribution in bushels, weight, or prices or some other common measure. **Box 2.1** presents two possible *aggregates* of apple and orange production.

The weighting in a price or quantity index is very important—a small change in the weight put on the production of communication equipment, for example, could have a big influence on the quantity index that we call GDP because communication equipment production has been such a fast-growing industry in the economy. As we will see, there are different views on the appropriate weights to use when creating macroeconomic aggregates, and so it is important to understand how the data are created in order for you to be able to form your own opinion.

BOX 2.1: QUANTITY INDEXES OF APPLES AND ORANGES

Case 1: Express each in terms of weight

2 apples $* \frac{1}{4}$ pound per apple $= \frac{1}{2}$ pounds of apples

$+$

3 oranges $* \frac{1}{5}$ pound per orange $= \frac{3}{5}$ pounds oranges

Total Production = 1.1 pounds of fruit

Case 2: Express each in terms of value

2 apples $* \$.50$ per apple $= \$1$ of apples

$+$

3 oranges $* \$.25$ per orange $= \$.75$ of oranges

Total Production = \$1.75 worth of fruit

2.3   THE CONSUMER PRICE INDEX

The most common measure of the U.S. *Aggregate Price Level* is the Consumer Price Index (the CPI). The CPI was designed to answer the following question: If the average household were to buy exactly the same bundle of goods and services today that it bought in year "x", how much more or less expensive would it be?

From this simple description, you may understand that the CPI is designed to measure *changes* in prices, and furthermore that it is specifically designed to measure *general changes in prices*, rather than the price of any one particular good or service.

As you know from **Section 2.2**, we have to aggregate (combine) the prices in the CPI bundle of goods by weighting them in some way. In the CPI, the weight on each price is equal to the fraction of total spending allocated to each good; that fraction is known as the *expenditure share* for each good.

2.3.1 Measurement of the CPI

The formula for the CPI is:

$$CPI_{t,baseyear} = \left\{ \frac{\text{Sum of prices in } t \text{ weighted by baseyear expenditure shares}}{\text{Sum of baseyear prices weighted by baseyear expenditure shares}} \right\} * 100,$$

where period t is the unit of *time* to which the price data refer—the unit of time can be a month, a year, or any other breakdown for which data are available. However, the expenditure shares are always calculated as the average in a particular year (the *base* year).

The base-year expenditure shares are calculated by conducting periodic surveys in which households report on their spending patterns: the expenditure share for each good or service is equal to its share of expenses for the *average urban household* in any given base year. In the U.S., the price data are collected monthly and are published about 2 weeks after the end of each month.

Figure 1 plots the annual level of the CPI over the period 1970 through mid-2003. The CPI is scaled in this case to equal an average of 100 over 1982-84. Because there is a general trend of inflation in the U.S. economy, prices before 1982 are generally below 100 and prices after 1982 are above 100.

FIGURE 1: U.S. CONSUMER PRICE INDEX (1982-4 = 100)

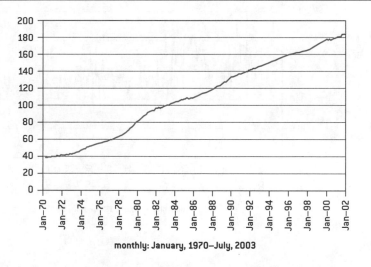

monthly: January, 1970–July, 2003

2.3.2 Inflation: The CPI Growth Rate

Rising prices is known as *inflation*, whereas a decline in prices is known as *deflation*. *Aggregate* U.S. inflation is measured as the growth rate of the CPI. Most people are concerned about CPI inflation, rather than about the *level* of the index.

If there is inflation in the CPI it means there is a general decline in the purchasing power of a dollar (it buys fewer things), and so we say that in *real terms* the dollar has less value if there is inflation. The "real terms" refers to the actual (real) number of goods and services for which the dollar can be exchanged. So, for example, one important question we will want to ask is whether or not wages—measured in dollars—are keeping up with inflation; the "real wage" will give us the purchasing power of the wage earned, and tell us how many (aggregate) goods or services can be bought given current (nominal) wages and current prices.

To measure aggregate inflation, we express the CPI in growth rates: The growth rate of a variable is equal to the *percentage change* in the variable; that is the change in the level relative to its size in the previous period.

Using mathematical notation in which putting a "dot" over a variable indicates we are looking at a growth rate, the formula for the CPI inflation rate is:

$$\dot{CPI}_t = \frac{CPI_{t,baseyear} - CPI_{t-1,baseyear}}{CPI_{t-1,baseyear}}$$

The *growth rate* of the CPI is shown in **Figure 2.**

FIGURE 2: CPI GROWTH RATE (1982–4 = 100)

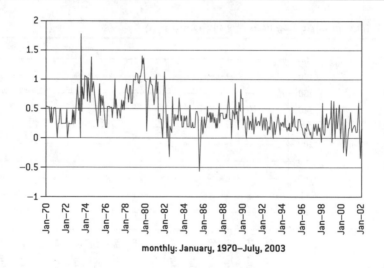

monthly: January, 1970–July, 2003

Box 2.2 shows the calculation of the CPI and of Inflation for the hypothetical country Xanadu, using 2003 as the base year. The levels of the CPI for December and January are not nearly as informative of economic conditions in Xanadu as is the growth rate: January inflation was 3.13%, assuming a base year of 2003. Notice that the base-year prices and expenditure shares used to calculate the inflation rate refer to the average month in the base year, whereas the "numerator" price data are for any particular month for which we want an inflation estimate.

BOX 2.2 CALCULATION OF PRICE INDEXES IN XANADU (2003 BASE YEAR)

Average Monthly

	2003	ES(2003)	2005	ES(2005)	2006	ES(2006)
Food and Rent	$1500	.4	$1700	.4	$1900	.4
Electronics	$500	.1	$400	.2	$300	.3
Other	$2000	.5	$2200	.4	$2700	.3

Monthly Survey of Prices

	Food and Rent	Electronics	Other
Dec., 2005	$1850	$350	$2600
Jan., 2006	$1900	$300	$2700

Calculation of CPI at 2003 base-year expenditure shares
Dec., 2005
100*(1850*.4+350*.1+2600*.5)/(1500*.4+500*.1+2000*.5) = 125.76
Jan., 2006
100*(1900*.4+300*.1+2700*.5)/(1500*.4+500*.1+2000*.5) = 129.70

January's monthly inflation rate, base year=2003: 3.13%
100* (129.70 – 125.76)/125.76 = 3.13

2.4   CRITICISMS OF THE CPI

Criticisms of the CPI come in two broad forms: those that find fault with the quality of the price data, and those that find fault with using expenditures-share weights from a base year.

2.4.1   Criticisms of Using Base-Year Expenditure-Shares

An index constructed with base-year weights such as the CPI is known as a *Laspeyres Index*. The strongest criticisms of the CPI are criticisms of Laspeyres Indexes in general.

2.4.1.1   Data Revisions When the Base Year is Changed

One problem with using a base-year weighting method is that every time the base year is "updated" it means changing the estimates of historical inflation rates even though the price data for those periods are unchanged—only the weights used in the index are being adjusted.

In order keep the expenditure weights in the CPI "up to date", the base-year is periodically changed: Until recently, the base-year changed every 10 years, but since 2002 the BLS has updated the expenditures shares every two years so that weights more accurately reflect current spending habits. (Of course, updating the expenditure shares makes CPI estimates for *previous* years less reflective of spending habits in *those* years, but most users of the inflation data are concerned about current conditions.)

Consequently, one critique of the CPI, and of Laspeyres indexes generally, is that data are *revised* (changed) every time the base-period gets updated.

BOX 2.3 CALCULATION OF PRICE INDEXES IN XANADU (2005 BASE YEAR)

Average Monthly

	2003	ES(2003)	2005	ES(2005)	2006	ES(2006)
Food and Rent	$1500	.4	$1700	.4	$1900	.4
Electronics	$500	.1	$400	.2	$300	.3
Other	$2000	.5	$2200	.4	$2700	.3

Monthly Survey of Prices

	Food and Rent	Electronics	Other
Dec., 2005	$1850	$350	$2600
Jan., 2006	$1900	$300	$2700

Calculation of CPI at 2005 base-year expenditure shares

Dec., 2005

$100*(1850*.4+350*.2+2600*.4)/(1700*.4+400*.2+2200*.4) = 112.80$

Jan., 2006

$100*(1900*.4+300*.2+2700*.4)/(1700*.4+400*.2+2200*.4) = 115.85$

January's monthly inflation rate, base year=2005: 2.70%

$100*(115.85 - 112.80)/112.80 = 2.70$

January's monthly inflation rate, base year=2003: 3.13%

2.4.1.2 Substitution Bias

One reason that expenditure weights change over time is that households substitute between similar types of goods.

The problem that changing expenditure-shares creates for the CPI is known as *substitution bias*. If a good becomes relatively more expensive, people may switch into a cheaper substitute; this means that expenditures shares may change over time in *response* to price changes. Thus, by holding expenditure shares constant, we fail to capture the total impact of price movements on the cost of living. This omission is known as substitution *bias* because it means that the standard CPI has a tendency to overstate inflation by assuming relatively large expenditures shares for inflationary items. Subsequent CPI revisions using more recent expenditure shares therefore tend to reduce historical inflation estimates because they use more recent expenditure share data.[1]

---

[1]Since 1999 the BLS has done it's best to account for substitution between similar goods within major groupings in the CPI (e.g. between different types of cars), but it keeps the expenditures shares on broad categories set equal to base-year values.

Box 2.3 illustrates how changing the base year can affect the inflation estimate for any period by comparing the January inflation rate for Xanadu using more recent (2005) expenditure shares with those calculated in Box 2.2. Expenditure shares on electronics have risen, and at the same time the weights on the relatively inflationary sector "other" have fallen—perhaps reflecting substitution away from inflationary and into lower-priced goods. The inflation estimate using the more recent expenditure weights is somewhat lower—2.7% rather than 3.13% measured aggregate price growth using historical spending patterns.

2.4.2 Criticisms of the price data

The criticisms of the CPI we've seen so far have concerned the indexing method used to calculate the CPI. Other criticisms revolve around the price data themselves.

2.4.2.1 Use of Urban Data

One criticism of the CPI is that the expenditure of an average urban household may not be representative of the U.S. as a whole. Moreover, households that live in the city do not necessarily *shop* there—many go to the suburbs to visit malls where prices are cheaper. In other words, the CPI may not even represent average urban consumers particularly well!

However, even if the level of the CPI is not very representative of average prices paid, CPI inflation may be a good indicator of general price increases if both urban and suburban prices tend to move together over time.

2.4.2.2 Hedonic Adjustment

To calculate the CPI, price data must be found that correspond to the types of goods available in the base year. Moreover, prices for goods in any year must be of the same quality as they were in the base year. Otherwise, we are measuring more than just changes in prices when we measure the CPI—we are also measuring changes in quality.

For example, if a good has improved in quality since the base year, then any price increase will also reflect quality improvements. The CPI estimate will therefore over-estimate inflation if the government collecting agent doesn't somehow "correct" the data for the quality improvement. That type of correction is known as *hedonic adjustment*.

So, for example, if we were to use 1992 base-year expenditure shares when calculating the 2006 CPI contribution of computers, we'd want to reduce the 2006 price estimate *by the amount of the price increase that reflected computer quality improvements since 1992*. This type of hedonic adjustment is clearly the right thing to do. The question is: how to do it?! How much better is a Pentium V computer than the 286 or 386 processor available in 1992? Should we make the comparison in terms of processing speed, or in terms of the *usefulness* in the gain of processing speed? And if the latter, how do we measure how much more of a processing speed improvement is valued as a quality improvement? You see, we need to know that in order to know if the increase in price paid is because we're willing to pay more for more quality, or because we're forced to pay more due to inflation.

The further back in time the base year, the more hedonic adjustments must be made in years since the base year. Thus the further back in time the base year, the more of the recent data have been "adjusted". Because hedonic adjustments are not without controversy, the further back in time the base year, the less some people trust the data.

On the other hand, the more recent the base year used to calculate the CPI, the more hedonic adjustments have to be done to the historical data (as they get further back in time from the base year), and so the less some people trust the historical data.

When it comes to hedonic adjustment, it seems you just can't pick a good base year! This problem has become particularly irksome in recent years of rapid technological change. Largely for this reason, but also because of the issue of substitution bias, the U.S. government has recently begun to experiment with a second method of estimating the aggregate price inflation: The chained CPI.

2.5   THE CHAINED CPI

The Chained CPI uses a very similar methodology as is used to calculate the regular CPI; the only difference is that the expenditure share weights in the Chained CPI change every year.

Because the expenditure share weights are updated annually, one advantage to the chain-weighted method is that it allows not only for changes in prices but also for changes in the composition of consumer expenditures—it eliminates the substitution bias of the Laspeyres index. A second advantage is that the chain-weighted estimate of CPI inflation will never be revised because there is no base year to change. And finally, the need for hedonic adjustment to prices is greatly reduced by the use of very recent expenditure shares.

Estimation of inflation in the chain-weighted CPI is quite straightforward: it is calculated as the average of the inflation rate using current expenditure shares and of the inflation rate using expenditure shares from the previous year.

The formula for inflation in the chain-weighted CPI in year t is

$$\dot{CPI_t} = .5 * \dot{CPI}_{t,baseyear=1} + .5 * \dot{CPI}_{t,baseyear=t-1}.$$

Where the inflation rates on the right hand side of the equation are calculated using the standard method for measuring CPI inflation shown in **Section 2.3**), but each with a different base-year for the expenditure shares.

The chain-weighted inflation estimate for the hypothetical economy of Xanadu is shown in **Box 2.4**. The chain-weighted estimate uses the same data used to calculate January inflation under the traditional CPI estimate, but it uses a combination of two base years to do so: current-year expenditure shares and previous-year expenditure shares.

Average Monthly

	2003	ES(2003)	2005	ES(2005)	2006	ES(2006)
Food and Rent	$1500	.4	$1700	.4	$1900	.4
Electronics	$500	.1	$400	.2	$300	.3
Other	$2000	.5	$2200	.4	$2700	.3

Monthly Survey of Prices

	Food and Rent	Electronics	Other
Dec., 2005	$1850	$350	$2600
Jan., 2006	$1900	$300	$2700

Calculation of CPI at 2006 base-year expenditure shares

Dec., 2005

100*(1850*.4+350*.3+2600*.3)/(1900*.4+300*.3+2700*.3) = 97.89

Jan., 2006

100*(1900*.4+300*.3+2700*.3)/(1900*.4+300*.3+2700*.3) = 100

January's monthly inflation rate, base year=2006: 2.15%

100* (100 − 97.89)/97.89 = 2.15

January's monthly inflation rate, base year=2005: 2.70%

January, 2006, chain-weighted inflation estimate: 2.43%

.5*2.15 + .5* 2.70 = 2.43%

2.5.1 Chain-Weighted Prices in the U.S. Economy

Consumer price inflation has been somewhat lower under the Chained measure than using the standard CPI because of the impact of substitution bias on the traditional measure. Wages are often tied to the CPI via cost-of-living-adjustments, as are social security benefits and many other types of income; because the chain-weighted measure has been less inflationary in recent years than the traditional measure, there are understandable political divisions over the adoption of the Chained measure as the official measure of changes in the U.S. cost of living. Currently, both measures are reported by the BLS, but the standard (base year expenditure shares) CPI is still the official measure of U.S. inflation.

2.6   GROSS DOMESTIC PRODUCT (GDP)

GDP is defined as the total quantity of final goods and services produced in the domestic economy in a given time period. This definition is carefully constructed so that the data will line up with a production function for the aggregate economy, so let's take a minute and think about what that definition implies:

- GDP is a *flow* of production—only what is produced in that time period. GDP is constructed in this way—to measure the *flow* of output—because our models of supply are constructed that way: Production functions give us information about new production, not the stock of things left over from previous time periods.
- GDP includes only "final" goods and services excludes anything used as an input into production, so that the data mirror the "output" side of the production function. [Inputs are measured in a different aggregate!]
- GDP measures production within the *domestic* economy, and so we will make sure to consider only *inputs* used in the domestic economy (e.g. domestic employment, regardless of citizenship, but excluding overseas employment of U.S. citizens).

2.6.1 GDP in Base-Year Prices

In most countries, and in the U.S. prior to 1996, the GDP estimate is created by weighting the quantities of every good and service produced within a given time period (usually a year, or a quarter of a year) by the price of that good or service in a base year. As with the expenditure shares in the traditional CPI, the base year gets changed every now and then to make sure that the price weights used are not too far out of line with ones that reflect current costs and tastes.

The formula for GDP in base-year prices is

$$GDP_{t, base\ year} = P_{base\ year}^{apples} * Q_t^{apples} + P_{bse\ year}^{computers} * Q_t^{compters} + \cdots$$

for all goods and services produced in period t

GDP *growth* is calculated in the same fashion as were growth rates in the CPI:

$$\dot{GDP_t} = \frac{GDP_{t, baseyear} - GDP_{t-1, baseyear}}{GDP_{t-1, baseyear}}$$

After reading the section on the CPI, the weaknesses of this (Laspeyres Index) measure of GDP should come as no surprise: changes in the base year lead to (sometimes dramatic) changes in the estimate of GDP growth; hedonic adjustment must be made for goods outside the base year, which makes the data less reliable the further away one gets from the base year.

In 1996 the U.S. officially switched to a chain-weighted measure of GDP.

2.6.2 GDP Growth in Chain-Weighted (C-W) Prices

2.6.2.1 Why the Move to C-W Measure?

There has been much more consensus in the U.S. about changing to a chain-weighted measure of GDP growth than there has been for adopting the chain-weighted measure of the CPI. The traditional CPI measures changes in prices *holding the standard of living constant*, whereas the

Chain-Weighted CPI is an index of prices of goods *actually purchased* in any time period—the two pieces of data measure different things and part of the debate is over which thing we want to measure.

In the case of GDP, however, we are simply trying to add up apples and oranges the best way we can, and by the mid-1990s there was consensus that the base-year price measure was not the best method. The reason for this consensus can be gleaned from **Figure 3**, which shows that some relative prices (for example, medical care and electronic equipment) were changing so dramatically that it made the GDP estimate extremely sensitive to the base year chosen. By comparison, changes in the expenditure shares used to calculate the CPI have changed must less dramatically over short time periods, and so there has been less to gain from switching the to chain-weighted CPI measure than there has been for the output aggregate.

FIGURE 3: PRICE INDEXES FOR SELECTED INDUSTRIAL AGGREGATIONS

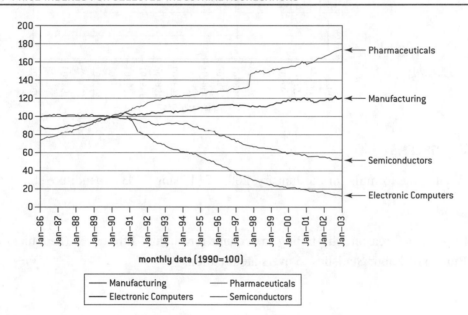

2.6.2.2 Estimating Chain-Weighted GDP Growth

Chain-weighted GDP is calculated using a Fisher *Quantity* Index that is analogous to the calculation of the chain-weighted CPI.

GDP growth is calculated as the average of GDP growth using price weights from the current year and from the previous year. [Note that base-year price data is annual, but the quantity data used to calculate GDP usually refer to a quarterly time period (four times a year).]

$$\dot{GDP_t} = .5*\dot{GDP}_{t,\text{baseyear}=1} + .5*\dot{GDP}_{t,\text{baseline}=t-1}.$$

As you can see in **Figure 4**, the U.S. was in the middle of a sustained period of strong economic growth when the BEA made the conversion to the chain-weighted measure in 1996. Nonetheless, the growth estimates in **Figure 4** are even lower than they had been using the (now defunct) base-year pricing method because some of the fastest-growing sectors of the economy (high-technology sectors) were also ones that had the steepest price declines. This reflects a type of substitution bias in the base-year GDP measure toward over-estimating GDP growth in the periods after the base year.

FIGURE 4: U.S. GDP GROWTH 1970Q1-2003Q2

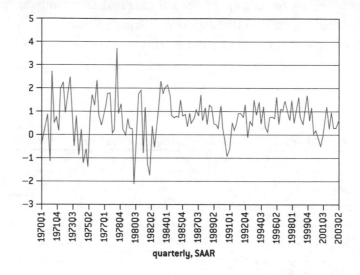

quarterly, SAAR

PRACTICE PROBLEMS

A. What is the formula for the January, 2005, CPI using 2003 expenditure shares?

B. Explain one reason why failing to account for quality differences (hedonics) might cause the Bureau of Labor Statistics to overstate inflation.

C. Explain one reason why the inflation estimate might be *lower* using the chain-weighted rather than the traditional Laspeyres (base-year weighting) CPI Index.

D. Explain one reason why inflation the inflation estimate might be *higher* using the chain-weighted rather than the traditional Laspeyres (base-year weighting) CPI Index.

A. January 2005 CPI (base-year 2003) is

$$CPI_{Jan2005,by=2003} = \left\{ \frac{\text{Sum of prices in January, 2005, weighted by 2003 expenditure shares}}{\text{Sum of 2003 prices weighted by 2003 expenditure shares}} \right\} *100,$$

B. The CPI measures the change in prices of goods available in the base year, using base-year expenditure shares on those goods as price weights. If only a superior-quality good is available, then it is likely worth more to consumers than would be the inferior-quality good; thus the price is likely higher than the base-year good would be at that time, and a CPI estimate that uses the price of the higher-quality good is thus overstating the cost of the bundle of goods purchased in the base year.

C. If households have substituted into cheaper goods over time, then expenditures shares on cheaper goods are larger in more recent years, making the CPI using recent expenditure shares smaller than the CPI using historic expenditures shares. The chain-weighted CPI uses current (very recent!) expenditure shares in its calculation.

D. Demand has risen for a good, causing its expenditure share to rise and also causing the price of that good to rise. Using more recent expenditure shares puts more weight on that expensive good, making the chain-weighted CPI estimate grow faster (be bigger).

HONORS APPENDIX 2

An Introduction to Math Tools Used in Economics

Although economists frequently use graphical depictions to illustrate the intuition behind a model, the real economic reasoning is always done using mathematics. In order to do even the most basic economic analysis, you must first become familiar with a few simple rules from calculus. You might think that you'd rather stick with graphical depictions than have to learn some calculus! In fact, however, the math tools you will need to do basic economic modeling are quite simple. Moreover, this mathematical introduction to how economics is really done should help you to understand some of the constraints on economic thinking—if you want nice clean mathematical solutions, you have to set up your model in certain ways. Of course, some math problems do not have solutions (e.g. what is four divided by zero?), and some math problems have more than one solution (e.g. what is the square root of four?). In this text we'll use only simple economic (mathematical) models that have unique solutions, but it should be clear that this will not always be the case.

We'll use calculus to derive some economic relationships later in the class, but for now we'll just get familiar with the technique. The next section describes how to find derivatives for one specific type of function often used in economic models. Later in the course we'll use the same techniques to mathematically derive labor- and capital-market demand and supply curves from a stylized (i.e. relatively simple!) macroeconomic model of production and utility.

2A.3   TAKING THE DERIVATIVE OF A FUNCTION

A derivative measures the impact of a marginal (small) change to one variable in a function. The *sign* of the derivative tells us whether that one variable has a positive or negative impact on the function; the *size* of the derivative tells the magnitude of the impact. This appendix shows you how to take the derivative of the types of functions we'll use in this text.

Exponential Function

Consider the following function, in which y is a function of variable x:

$$y = f(x) = a \cdot x^n$$

In this example, increases in x clearly have a positive impact on y if a is positive. The magnitude of a marginal (small) increase in x is found using the following formula:

$$\text{Derivative of } y \text{ with respect to } x = f'(x) = a \cdot n \cdot x^{n-1}$$

The rule is the same every single time—a is unaffected by x, so leave it alone. Then multiply x by its exponent, and reduce the power of the exponent on x by one.

To illustrate, consider two mathematical examples:

- $y = f(x) = 2 \cdot x^3$
  - $f'(x) = 2 \cdot 3 \cdot x^2 = 6 \cdot x^2$

and

- $z = f(x,y) = 2 \cdot x \cdot y^{\frac{1}{3}}$
  - $f'(x) = 2 \cdot 1 \cdot x^0 \cdot y^{\frac{1}{3}} = 2 \cdot 1 \cdot 1 \cdot y^{\frac{1}{3}} = 2 \cdot y^{\frac{1}{3}}$

2A.3 THE TOTAL DERIVATIVE

If the function depends on more than one variable, then you might be interested in knowing what happens if all the variables change at once; that is referred to as taking the "total derivative" of the function. In that case, you just add up the partial derivatives with respect to each moving variable, multiplied by the amount each variable changes.

For example, consider the following function:

$$z = f(x,y) = 2 \cdot x \cdot y^{\frac{1}{3}}$$

The total derivative (Δz) is equal to

$$\Delta z = f'_x(x,y) \cdot \Delta x + f'_y(x,y) \cdot \Delta y$$

$$\Delta z = 2 \cdot 1 \cdot y^{\frac{1}{3}} \cdot \Delta x + \frac{1}{3} \cdot 2 \cdot x \cdot y^{\frac{1}{3}-\frac{3}{3}} \cdot \Delta y = 2 \cdot y^{\frac{1}{3}} \cdot \Delta x + \frac{2}{3} \cdot x \cdot y^{-\frac{2}{3}} \cdot \Delta y$$

2A.3 USING TOTAL DIFFERENTIATION TO CALCULATE THE GROWTH RATE

The growth rate of a function is equal to the total derivative divided by the level—after reading this section, it will be easy to see the method used to calculate the expression for growth rates of chain-weighted CPI and GDP presented in this chapter.

To continue with the previous example, the growth rate of function z is defined as

$$\frac{\Delta z}{z} = \frac{2 \cdot y^{\frac{1}{3}}}{2 \cdot x \cdot y^{\frac{1}{3}}} \cdot \Delta x + \frac{\frac{2}{3} \cdot x \cdot y^{-\frac{2}{3}}}{2 \cdot x \cdot y^{\frac{1}{3}}} \cdot \Delta y = \frac{1}{x} \Delta x + \frac{1}{3} * \frac{1}{y} \Delta y$$

which is the weighted sum of the growth rates of the components:

$$\frac{\Delta z}{z} = \frac{\Delta x}{x} + \frac{1}{3} \cdot \frac{\Delta y}{y}$$

Or, using the notation from the chapter,

$$\dot{z} = \dot{x} + \frac{1}{3} \cdot \dot{y}$$

We'll use this formula throughout the course to calculate growth rates of functions such as the chain-weighted CPI, chain-weighted GDP, and our production function.

SOME MACROECONOMIC DATA

The CPI and GDP data are put together so that they can be used by analysts and policymakers, recognizing that not all users of the data will be interested in the same price or quantity aggregates. This chapter discusses the presentation of the CPI and GDP data as well as some of the other key economic data that make the stock market jump, affect election campaigns, and are the bell-weathers of U.S. economic conditions generally.

3.1   SEASONALLY ADJUSTED AND ANNUALIZED DATA

3.1.1   Seasonal Adjustment

Macroeconomic data are nearly always presented in a "seasonally adjusted" format. Seasonal adjustment removes the usual variations in the data that are typical, or "normal", for any particular month or quarter in an *average* year.

We know for example that retail sales are normally higher in December than for the average month (because of holidays and inventory sales), that there are normally more autos produced in the fall than any other season of the year (to introduce the new model year), that there is usually more demand for gasoline in the summertime than any other time of the year (summer vacations), and so on.

If you were to read that auto production and retail sales rose at the end of last year but gasoline sales fell, you would want to know if that was just normal variation because of seasonal things, or if the movements in the data were *abnormal-*

ly large. Seasonal adjustment of the data removes the (estimated) normal variations that will occur over the year.

If you already know a lot about every industry in the economy, of course, you don't need the government economists to "seasonally adjust" the data for you, but it is much easier to let them do it! Almost all government data in the U.S. are seasonally adjusted, although some non-seasonally adjusted data are available for use by industry analysts and economists that prefer to do their own seasonal adjustment based on their own expertise or views of what is "normal".

FIGURE 1: U.S. CONSTRUCTION EMPLOYMENT (THOUSANDS)

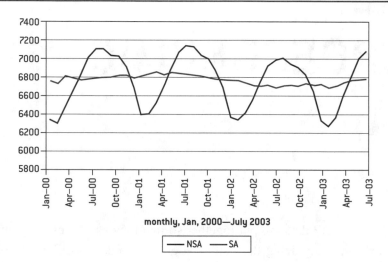

monthly, Jan, 2000—July 2003

— NSA — SA

Figure 1 plots monthly employment in the U.S. Construction industry for the period January 2000 through July 2003; both the non-seasonally adjusted (NSA) and seasonally adjusted (SA) data are shown. Employment in the Construction industry has a strong seasonal pattern, with a large upswing in employment in the summer months and a downswing during the winter (as might be expected!). The SA data remove the usual seasonal variation from the Construction employment data by subtracting off the average seasonally-related increase in the summer, and adding that same amount to the SA data in the winter months.

The SA data are much "smoother" in **Figure 1** than the NSA data because so much of the variation in employment in this industry is related to seasonal, rather than cyclical, factors. If all the movement in the monthly data could be explained by seasonal factors, then the seasonally adjusted data would be exactly the same in every month of a year.

The sum of all seasonal adjustment factors within any year is equal to zero because the sum of deviations from the average is by definition equal to zero; in other words, the *seasonal factors* sum to zero over the course of the year.

Figure 2 plots the monthly change in total U.S. manufacturing employment. Note that the SA data do not always move in the same direction as the NSA data. For example, the employment report for January 2003 showed a fairly steep decline in employment, but because employment usually falls by even *more* than that in the average January, the BLS added a strong positive seasonal factor when creating the SA data; consequently, the SA employment data for

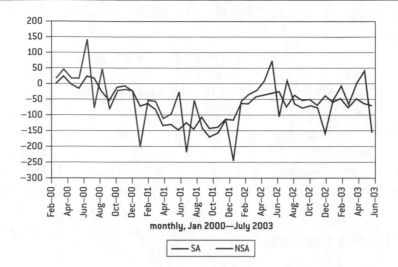

monthly, Jan 2000—July 2003

January *rose* while the NSA data *fell*. People who understood the data knew that the publicized employment increase that January was a result of the seasonal factor rather than actual increase in the number of people with jobs because that fact was highlighted in the Bureau of Labor Statistics employment report for that month.

Although there are macroeconomic models that do so, the standard macro model that we will present does not (yet?!) attempt to explain seasonal fluctuations. Consequently, seasonally-adjusted data are most appropriate for comparison with our model.

3.1.2 Annualized Data

The "frequency" of a piece of data refers to the time period that the data cover. GDP for example comes out at a quarterly frequency (four times a year), and refers to the flow of production that occurs over particular 3-month blocks of time. Retail Sales data comes out at a monthly frequency, and estimates of the total U.S. stock of capital goods used in production is estimated at an annual frequency. Economists would love it if all data came at a monthly frequency, but to collect so many data at a monthly frequency with any degree of accuracy would be very expensive and would probably not be worth the cost to the taxpayer.

To make data at different frequencies comparable, therefore, it is convenient to *annualize* the data, which means to infer from the current period information what the level or growth rate for the year would be if current conditions were to continue. Seasonal adjustment is of course essential prior to putting the data in annual terms.

The formula for conversion of seasonally-adjusted data into annual *levels* is quite straightforward: simply multiply the data by its annual frequency. In the case of quarterly data for the third quarter of 2003, the formula would be:

$$Data_{2003Q3, annual\ level} = Data_{2003Q3,SA} * 4.$$

The following formula is used to calculate the implied annual *growth rate* of 2003Q3 data, where the term "SAAR" indicates that the data are "seasonally adjusted and at annual rates":

$$\dot{Data}_{2003Q3,SAAR} = \left[\left(1 + \dot{Data}_{2003Q3,SA}\right)^4 - 1\right] * 100.$$

Whereas the conversion formula for monthly data would be

$$\dot{Data}_{Jan2003,\ annual\ rate} = \left[\left(1 + \dot{Data}_{Jan2003,SA}\right)^{12} - 1\right] * 100.$$

and so on, where the "dot" above a piece of data indicates as always that the term is expressed in growth rates.

3.2 THE CPI AND ITS COMPONENTS

The CPI is created using base-year expenditure shares and monthly price data. Prices are collected for thousands of commodities, and each commodity price is adjusted using its own seasonal factor before the data are aggregated into the seasonally-adjusted measure of the price index. The first estimate of the monthly measure of the CPI comes out about 2 weeks after the end of each month.

TABLE A. PERCENT CHANGES IN CPI FOR URBAN CONSUMERS (CPI-U)

Expenditure Category	Changes from Preceding Month 2003							Seasonally Adjusted Compound Annual Rate 3-mos. Ended	Unadjusted 12-mos. Ended
	Jan.	Feb.	Mar.	Apr.	May	June	July	July '03	July '03
All Items	.3	.6	.3	-.3	.0	.2	.2	1.3	2.1
Special Indexes									
Energy	4.0	5.9	4.6	-4.6	-3.1	.8	.4	-7.1	9.0
Food	-.2	.7	.2	-.1	.3	.4	.1	3.4	2.1
All Items less food and energy	.1	.1	.0	.0	.3	.0	.2	1.9	1.5

Source: Bureau of Labor Statistics, August 2003

The Bureau of Labor Statistics publishes price indexes for 200 subcomponents of the CPI, but it is most common to look at the CPI data in the way they are presented in **Table A**: The overall CPI and three "special" categories Energy, Food, and what is known as the *Core CPI* (all items less food and energy). Because food and energy prices are sometimes strongly affected by factors that are not general to the whole economy (such as droughts or unrest in the Middle East), the Core CPI is often considered to be the best indicator of trends in the cost of living.

Each month, the BLS press release will focus attention on particularly noteworthy changes in prices that may have occurred in any commodities, as well as discuss whether atypical seasonal movements (unusually warm weather, unusually late Easter, and so on) have had any particularly significant influence on that month's price measure.

The CPI data in **Table A** are presented in terms of percentage changes for each of the last seven months, the total percentage change over the last three months (at an annual rate), and the percentage change over the last twelve months. The data for the 12-month percentage change need not be seasonally adjusted, of course, because one is comparing prices in the same season in different years.

3.3   GDP AND ITS AGGREGATE EXPENDITURE COMPONENTS

In constructing the chained GDP estimate, quantities are weighted by their prices. But many goods have more than one price, depending on the purchaser (households pay the retail price, firms a bulk or wholesale price, and governments, that often buy in even larger quantities may pay yet another price). Moreover, the seasonal spending patterns for households, firms, and governments may also be quite different from one another. In short, different prices and seasonal factors will be used to depending on the group responsible for *expenditures* for each good, and organization of the data into expenditure categories is necessary before chain-weighting can begin.

Because *users* of macroeconomic data are concerned about the behavior of these different spending groups, the GDP report will usually give information about not only chained GDP but also about chained estimates of sales to each *Aggregate Expenditure* category.

3.3.1   The Aggregate Expenditures Approach to Measuring GDP

Everything that is produced within a given time period is either bought during that same time period or put into inventories. That means that one way to present the GDP data is as the sum of spending by everyone in the economy, including any change-in-inventory expenses; this method of organizing GDP data is known as the *Aggregate Expenditures Approach.*

Because the Expenditures Approach to measuring GDP relates to the demand (expenditure) side of an economic model, the BEA organizes the quarterly GDP data by expenditure categories that correspond to standard macroeconomic models like the one we'll use in this text. In particular, we assume that households behave differently from firms, and that households and firms behave differently from state, local, and federal governments, and finally that foreigners behave differently than people living in the U.S.

In the terminology of the GDP release, purchases by households are called *Personal Consumption*, business purchases are called *Investment (Fixed Investment + Changes in Inventories)*, purchases by the public sector are called *Government Consumption and Investment*, and sales to foreigners are called *Exports*.

The Aggregate Expenditure Approach to organizing GDP data satisfies the following accounting definition:

$$\text{GDP} = \text{Personal Consumption} + \text{Fixed Investment} + \text{Change in Business Inventories} + \text{Government} + \text{Exports} - \text{Imports,}$$

where in order to make sure that domestic spending is equal to domestic production, we must subtract off imported goods that were purchased by households, firms, and public enterprises.

3.3.1.1 The Advance, Preliminary, and Final GDP Estimates

Information used to calculate GDP by the Aggregate Expenditures approach comes from a great variety of sources. For example, monthly surveys of retail establishments give detailed information on the value of sales of many types of commodities; the BEA then uses rules of thumb to determine which commodities are sold to households (Consumption) and which to firms (Investment). Monthly price data are used to estimate the chain-weighted level of output for each commodity, and each commodity is seasonally adjusted using its own seasonal factor before putting it into the aggregate formula for real GDP. If monthly price or expenditure data do not exist, then the BEA will extrapolate from the last observed (usually annual) bit of price information, using the last piece of observed data as a starting point and then assuming that expenditure on that particular good is moving in the same direction as expenditures on other related goods.

It takes a lot of economists and industry analysts to put together a quarterly estimate of GDP because there is so much information to process and so much industry expertise required to do it. Moreover, a lot of the data that are used sort of trickle in over time—much of it *after* the BEA publishes its first GDP press release. As a consequence, GDP estimates get revised on a regular basis, and those revisions can sometimes be substantial.

The first estimate of GDP in any quarter is released at the end of the first month in the following quarter; at that point the BEA has sufficient information to make what is called the "Advance Estimate of GDP". That estimate is revised one month later in the "Preliminary Estimate of GDP". The revision is based on revisions to the monthly CPI and sales data, etc, used in the first release, but it also reflects new information on international trade and wholesale trade data that are only available to the BEA with a two-month lag.

At the end of each quarter, the "Final Estimate of GDP" is published for the *previous* quarter (e.g. the final estimate for fourth-quarter GDP is published in March of the following year); there is usually not much of a revision between the Preliminary and the Final release, as it is just a matter of getting more complete information on data that were already available for the Preliminary report.

3.3.1.2 The Annual GDP Revision

In addition to the monthly revisions during the following quarter, the BEA uses annual data to completely revise some of the estimates made over the previous year. Each summer, the Census publishes its report on annual investment and inventory accumulation by firms in the *previous* year.

For example in the summer of 2007, the Census will publish the 2006 data for total Investment and Changes in Inventories. That number will result in a revision of the 2006 Investment and GDP data, but may also cause some revision to the 2005 estimate as well because the data will add to the information about 2005 end-of-year stocks of investment goods and inventories. Furthermore, it changes the "starting point" used to infer 2007 investment expenditures, and so there will also be another revision to the quarterly 2007 estimates that will already have been made. These annual revisions can sometimes be quite substantial when the economy is in transition because it means that the rules-of-thumb used to extrapolate quarterly movements from annual data may not have been appropriate.

As you might imagine, considerable effort is underway at U.S. government agencies to try to reduce the size of revisions, so that economists and policymakers make real-time use of the data with more confidence. At the same time, policymakers and analysts will look at some of the other indicators we discuss later in this chapter to help them predict the revisions to GDP.

3.3.1.3 The GDP Press Release

Data in the BEA press release on GDP are presented in chain-weighted growth rates, and all quarterly data are seasonally adjusted. Table B shows some of the data included in a sample GDP publication.

TABLE B: GDP DATA (SOURCE: BEA)

[Quarters seasonally adjusted at annual rates]

	2003	2004/r/	2004:Q3	2004:Q4/r/
Gross domestic product (GDP)	3.0	4.4	4.0	3.8
Personal consumption expenditures	3.3	3.8	5.1	4.2
Durable goods	7.4	6.7	17.2	3.9
Nondurable goods	3.7	4.6	4.7	5.9
Services	2.2	2.8	3.0	3.4
Gross private domestic investment	4.4	13.2	2.4	13.3
Fixed investment	5.1	10.3	8.8	10.5
Nonresidential	3.3	10.6	13.0	14.5
Structures	-5.6	1.4	-1.1	2.1
Equipment and software	6.4	13.6	17.5	18.4
Residential	8.8	9.7	1.6	3.4
Change in private inventories	.....	.....	.....	.....
Net exports of goods and services	.....	.....	.....	.....
Exports	1.9	8.6	6.0	3.2
Imports	4.4	9.9	4.6	11.4
Government consumption expenditures and gross investment	2.8	1.9	0.7	0.9
Addenda:				
Gross national product (GNP)	3.3	4.3	4.0	3.5

r Revised.

Note that changes in Inventories plus Fixed Investment together make up the broader expenditure category "Gross Private Domestic Investment" because both are business expenses. (Inventory data are always expressed in "changes" because only the flow of new inventories is counted; by convention, growth rates of the change in inventories are not included in the release.) Household expenditures on residential structures are included in this category because they are a type of business investment (into household equity) made by landowners. However, because *firm* investments in structures may behave quite differently from *household* investments in structures, the BEA reports each separately.

In general, the BEA provides separate information for expenditure categories for which we have distinct economic theories and explanations: household spending on refrigerators and cars (durable goods that don't have to be replaced if times are bad) is affected differently by economic events than is spending on food (nondurables) or education (services); state and local government outlays are affected by different factors than federal spending. A great deal of detailed data is also available from the BEA for use by economists with a more focused interest in a particular industry or spending category.

The BEA also presents data on something called Gross *National* Product (GNP is the last line in Table B). GNP measures the flow per unit of time of all goods and services produced by U.S. *citizens*—it is related to the GDP number but adds the production of U.S. citizens living abroad and subtracts that of foreigners living in the U.S.

3.3.2 The Income Approach to Measuring GDP

The BEA constructs a second measure of domestic production as a check to that calculated using the Aggregate Expenditures approach; this second measure is calculated by adding up the incomes, including corporate profit, of everyone who contributes to domestic production. In principal, the nominal value of current GDP—GDP calculated by the Aggregate Expenditures approach using current prices as weights—should exactly equal aggregate income earned by firms and individuals (nominal GDP calculated by the incomes approach). In practice the two measures do not yield exactly the same number; the gap between the two is one indication of methodological, reporting, and accounting problems in either or both of the two measures.

3.4 SOME MONTHLY ECONOMIC INDICATORS

As indicated in **Section 3.3**, the "Final" GDP Release comes out one month after the end of each quarter, and is subject to substantial revision thereafter. Consequently, policymakers, participants in the stock market, and other economic analysts, look to monthly indicators to help them make better estimates of GDP before official estimates are published; this activity is known as economic forecasting.

This section reviews some of the monthly indicators that are most closely related to GDP or its components. Press releases of these data often have big (if temporary!) impacts on the stock market, and almost always make front-page news in business sections and on news-service home pages, so it is a good idea to have some sense of what the data are.

3.4.1 Retail Sales

The Bureau of the Census conducts monthly surveys of retail sales at large firms. Retail trade data are first released about 2 weeks after the end of each month and are subsequently revised in each of the following three months. These data are important inputs into the advance estimate of GDP and into the Consumption component in particular. Because revisions to the Retail Sales data are published relatively early in the month they are also good indicators of upcoming GDP revisions.

3.4.2 Wholesale Trade

The Wholesale Trade data include end-of-month inventory stocks as well as shipments by producers to distributors, firms and households. The data are collected by the Bureau of the Census and are the result of monthly surveys of "large" firms; these are firms for which inventories or shipments are greater than a defined level (these levels vary by industry type). The data are published about six weeks after the end of each month.

One closely-watched piece of wholesale trade data is the Inventory-Shipments (or Inventory-Sales) ratio, although interpretation of those data is particularly tricky. Consider for example a decrease in the Inventory-Shipments ratio. If the ratio is falling, it may suggest that demand is rising faster than production (the denominator is rising as shipments increase, and the numerator is falling because goods are being sold out of inventory since production can't keep up). On the other hand, the Inventory-Shipments ratio may be falling because firms anticipate a future *decline* in demand, and so they are trimming inventories now. The first and second scenarios have opposite implications for the economy! Consequently, Interpretation of the Wholesale Trade data is usually made in connection with reference to other pieces of economic data (such as employment).

The shipments data from the Wholesale Trade release are used in the construction of the GDP estimate, with rules of thumb used to allocate the shipments across expenditure categories; these rules of thumb are important as not all shipments are of "final" goods and services but are rather intermediate goods used in the *production* of final goods. For example, some computers are sold directly to households or firms as final goods, whereas some computers are installed in autos or airplanes which are themselves sold as final goods.

The wholesale data for the last month of each quarter are released after the Advance GDP estimate; that last month of data is a significant factor affecting revisions that appear in the Preliminary GDP release. There is an additional revision each spring as the result of the annual Census survey.

It is noteworthy that Inventory-Shipments ratios have generally been falling since the 1990s, when information-sharing technologies began reducing the level of inventories firms needed to meet sudden increases in demand for their products; this downward trend made changes in the Inventory-Shipments ratio particularly difficult to interpret during the economic recession and slow recovery of the early 2000s (**Figure 3**). For example, the Inventory-Shipments ratio in the summer of 2003 was low by historical standards, but lies quite a bit above the level that would have prevailed if the downward trend in the Inventory-Shipments ratio had continued through the recession.

FIGURE 3: U.S. MANUFACTURING INVENTORY/SHIPMENTS RATIO

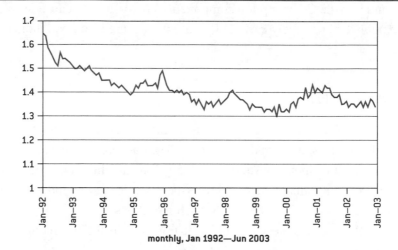

monthly, Jan 1992—Jun 2003

3.4.3 Employment

The most timely and carefully-watched monthly indicator is the Employment report, which is published by the Bureau of Labor Statistics (BLS) about a week after the end of each month. The numbers in the report are based on a survey of large firms which are representative of most industries and regions in the U.S. (excluding farming).

The BLS press release that accompanies the Employment data will emphasize if seasonal factors have had a large influence on the reported numbers—that is often the case, as seasonality is such a big component of changes in employment in many industries (see Section 3.1). The BLS will also point out if any revisions to the previous month have been substantial, which, as with any firm survey data, is also frequently the case. The employment numbers for each month of a given year are revised the following year, using annual Census and personal income data.

Employment data are one of the most important inputs into the GDP calculation. Actual production data are available for relatively few industries on a quarterly basis, but employment data are much more widely available. The BEA uses the employment data, in combination with assumptions about production functions for each industry, to *infer* the level of output produced by those workers. That is the best guess of GDP for many industries until the annual GDP revision.

3.4.4 Personal Income

The Bureau of Economic Analysis publishes the Personal Income report with a two-month delay; there are revisions over the following two months and then of course annually with the collection of tax data. A great deal of the information in the report is "old news"—payroll income, for example, can be estimated from the BLS' employment report. However, the Personal Income release also includes an estimate of monthly expenditures on consumer services, which is new and economically meaningful information.

The BEA report breaks consumption spending into three categories: durables, nondurables, and services. Durables tend to fall most steeply during recessions, and subsequently to rise most during booms—this is because it is easier to delay purchases of durable goods (like cars and refrigerators) until times are "good" again. The durables and nondurables consumption data are "old news" because they can be inferred from the Census' Retail Sales publication. The new information is in the consumption of services: Consumer Services make up more than half of total consumption expenditures, and are therefore a significant indicator of economic activity as well as a significant factor in the GDP estimate.

3.4.5 Index of Industrial Production

The Federal Reserve Board puts out a monthly measure of industrial activity known as the Index of Industrial Production (IP). This index is put together using the same information used to calculate GDP, but on a much smaller scale; it includes only manufacturing and utilities and excludes services and agricultural production. The IP index adds up the quantities of manufacturing goods, mining, and utilities; the index weights are the share each sector contributes in the total production of industrial goods—known as "value added". Value added shares change over time as the composition of the industrial sector changes so that, for example, the high-tech sector (computers, communications equipment, and semiconductors) has more weight in the index now than it did twenty years ago, whereas the textile sector now has a smaller weight. Nonetheless, most of the year-to-year changes in the production weights are fairly small, which means that most of the short-term movements in IP reflect changes in quantity *produced* rather than changes in the *composition* of the manufacturing sector.

The index is published about 2 weeks after the end of each month, along with revisions for the previous three months. There are also revisions each summer that incorporate annual Census survey results.

Although the industrial sector makes up less than a quarter of U.S. GDP, movements in the manufacturing component of the IP index are loosely correlated with movements in GDP—whenever manufacturing is in decline (growth is negative), GDP is in decline . Analysts therefore closely watch movements in the IP index as an indicator not only of industrial, but of general economic activity.

The IP release also includes the Federal Reserve Board estimate of manufacturing capacity utilization—the degree to which firms are producing at their potential; this is an indicator of the direction of future pricing and of capital investment decisions.

You can see why the IP index gets so much press! It is a monthly indicator that is highly correlated with overall economic activity (GDP), it gives us timely information about the direction of changes in production of manufactured Investment and Consumption goods and the estimates of capacity utilization included in the release give us information about scarcity and pricing pressures.

PRACTICE PROBLEMS

    A. Write the relationship between GDP and the sum of its Aggregate Expenditure Components.

    B. Use your answer to Part A to explain why the January, 2006, sale of a bike produced in 2005 will have no impact on first quarter GDP in 2006.

    C. Use your answer to Part A to explain why the January, 2006, sale in California of an imported bike will have no impact on first quarter GDP in 2006.

    D. What is nominal GDP? Why do we economists care more about real GDP than about nominal GDP?

SUGGESTED ANSWERS

    A. The Aggregate Expenditure Components of GDP are:

$$GDP = C + \text{Fixed } I + G + X - M + \text{change inventories}$$

    B. $\Delta GDP = \Delta C + \Delta inv = +bike - bike = 0$

    C. $\Delta GDP = \Delta C - \Delta M = +bike - bike = 0$

    D. Nominal GDP is the value of production of all goods and services in a given time period. There are many reasons economists are more concerned with real GDP than with nominal GDP: Because we care about output of a production function, we care about output per person rather than prices paid per person, because quantities produced gives us information about the amount of employment that is needed, and because we want data to correspond to model in which P and Q jointly determined but in which they are determined separately from one another.

APPENDIX 3

Problems with U.S. Employment Data

Employment and Unemployment data are published by the Bureau of Labor Statistics (BLS). The BLS collects employment data in three ways: 1. It collects monthly payroll data from large firms in many industries, 2. It collects weekly unemployment insurance claims data from around the country, and 3. It conducts a telephone survey asking people about their employment (or unemployment) situation.

Estimating Employment

The BLS attempts to get a representative sampling of industries in its monthly payroll survey, so that the fraction of each type of industry sampled roughly corresponds to its share of total production. The BLS makes no attempt to sample every firm in every industry however, but collects information instead from a few large firms in each sector of the economy. This collection method is fine if large firms behave the same way that small firms do.

In fact, it seems that small firms do not always follow the same cyclical pattern as large firms in the same industry. Small firms are often start-ups, or new entrants to the market. Start-up employment rises quickly as the economy comes out of a downturn, whereas large firms that have been hoarding labor do not have to hire more workers in order to increase production. Thus actual employment may be rising even if large-firm employment is not, and so the payroll survey data make it look as though the employment situation is worse than it is.

Rather than attempt to survey all firms in the economy, the BLS complements its payroll survey with a survey of households. In the Household Survey, the BLS collects information on the number of people in the household with and without jobs as well as the nature of the jobs they hold—whether they are permanent or part-time positions, salaried or wage, and so on. The survey is unbiased in the sense that respondents may be employed in any type of industry or in any size firm, and so it is not subject to the same criticisms as the Payroll Survey. Unfortunately, the size of the survey is rather small, and so it is unlikely to be a representative sampling of the entire working population.

Because of the larger sample size, most economists use the data from the payroll survey as their best U.S. employment measure.

Estimating Unemployment

The Household Survey collects data on the number of household members that are out of work but seeking employment; it also collects information on household members that have given up looking for employment (dropped out of the labor force) as well as why they have left the labor force—to get reeducated, to raise children, because they feel they are unemployable, or whatever the cause. Information about the *reasons* for unemployment are important to economists—it is often the case that Payroll Employment estimates will be unchanged but Unemployment estimates will fall, suggesting that workers are leaving the labor force; if workers are leaving the labor force because the returns to working are too low, that has a different economic implication than if they have left the workforce because search costs are too high to make it worthwhile to keep searching, or if alternatively they are leaving the labor force because returns from getting re-educated are so high.

In other words, the Household Survey tells us exactly what we want to know about Unemployment. Unfortunately, the small sample size makes it an unreliable estimate of the fraction of people unemployed in the United States.

A second method of collecting unemployment data is by measuring the number of people that make claims for national unemployment insurance (UI). Not all workers are eligible to collect unemployment insurance, however, and so the "claims" data tend to underestimate total unemployment.

One reason the UI claims data underestimates unemployment is that workers lose eligibility to collect the benefit after three months of unemployment, though this deadline is usually extended by Congress during economic downturns. Even if the deadline is extended, however, the long-term unemployed will eventually stop showing up in the UI claims data. Consequently, it is not unusual for the Unemployment (claims) data to *fall* (improve) in the middle of an economic downturn, even while the Household Survey estimate of unemployment is *rising* (worsening). Both pieces of data are flawed, and so if they are not moving in the same way it is hard to know which to prefer.

Because of its inclusion of the long-term unemployed that are still looking for jobs, most economists prefer to use the household survey as their measure or U.S. employment despite its small sample size.

THE PRODUCTION FUNCTION AND THE MARKETS FOR CAPITAL AND LABOR

We are now ready to derive the (Aggregate) Supply side of the model (though we'll put off graphing Aggregate Supply for a few more chapters yet!). For that, we need to specify the inputs into the production function as well as model the markets for those inputs.

4.1 THE INPUTS INTO THE PRODUCTION FUNCTION

The inputs into the aggregate production function are defined as the contribution of labor inputs (L), the contribution of capital inputs (K), and "all other inputs", which are grouped in a category known variously as "total factor productivity" (TFP) or "multifactor productivity" (MFP); we will use the latter term throughout the text. The output from the production function is equal to (real, chain-weighted) GDP.

The labor input is fairly straightforward: it is the number of hours worked by everyone in the labor force. We'll take some time to be clear about the other two inputs before proceeding to discuss the production function itself.

4.1.1 The Capital Stock

GDP is a flow of production over a given time period. While labor is hired every period, and so has a flow concept, the capital used to produce goods and services may have been made and purchased many years ago or it may be brand new.

We define new capital as "Investment" and old capital as the "capital stock" or simply by the letter "K". K is just the sum of all the investments that were made over all of history, minus any depreciation in the capital through wear and tear or obsolescence—it is the stock of all Investment currently available for use in production.

Firms are required to file an annual report with the Bureau of the Census every year that reports the amount of new Investments made that year as well as their estimate of capital depreciation incurred; from these data the BEA is able to make an estimate of K that corresponds to that in our model.

Many models will also include government capital investments in the aggregate production function, and of course there are also government investments into roads, utilities, and so on, that may also be included in the total U.S. capital stock. We will ignore government capital in this text because the decision to invest in government capital is not driven by the perfectly competitive pressures that determine firm investment levels.

4.1.2   MFP

Multifactor Productivity is an input that augments the usefulness of the capital and labor inputs in production. That is a rather vague definition! What economists have in mind when they refer to MFP are things like patents and designs, managerial skill, and things that generally affect the efficiency of *both* the capital and the labor inputs. That is why it is known as *multi* or (more optimistically!) *total* factor productivity—because it affects the productivity of all the (multiple) *measured* inputs that affect production. We will talk more about MFP in chapter 5.

4.2   THE PRODUCTION FUNCTION

In symbolic form, the production function can be written

$$GDP = f (MFP, L, K)$$

The right-hand side of the equation reads "is a function of the quantity of MFP, L and K" and the function, when specified, tells us the *contribution* of each input in the creation of GDP.

The production function that we'll use in this class must have certain characteristics in order for it to be able to explain the data that we observe in the real world. Some of the assumptions we'll make for our production function include

- Diminishing returns to K and to L

- Exogenous determination of MFP

- K investments affect GDP with a lag

4.2.1 Assumption #1: Diminishing Returns to K and L

Diminishing returns is the assumption that, holding all other inputs constant, an increase in one variable will cause output to increase by less and less the more the input increases. Consider for example a firm that has a capital good of one cash register and a labor input of one worker. If a second worker is hired, there is undoubtedly more output. However, there are now two workers using the one cash register; and they get in the way of each other and reduce each other's individual productivity relative to when the initial worker had sole access to the machine. Total output has risen, but the productivity per worker is lower. That fall in labor productivity as L increases is known as *diminishing returns to labor*. The example clearly only applies if the capital input is unchanged—if you doubled both workers and cash registers, output would double and productivity per worker would be unchanged.

Figure 1 plots GDP as a function of L under the assumption of diminishing returns, with GDP on the vertical axis and L on the horizontal. GDP increases the more we increase L, but the ratio of the change in GDP relative to the change in L is falling—graphically, this means that the *slope* of the production function is getting flatter.

FIGURE 1

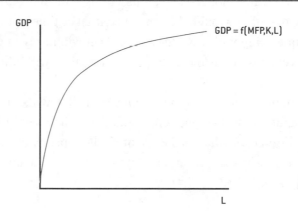

The assumption of diminishing returns to both the labor and capital input is fairly natural, but also extremely important. The more workers a firm hires, the less productive is each one (holding K and MFP constant) and so the less the firm is willing to pay per additional unit of employment. Similarly, the more capital a firm purchases, the less productive it is (holding L and MFP constant); thus the firm is only willing to buy more K if its price is lower as well. The assumption of diminishing returns, in short, is a crucial assumption behind our understanding of firm demand for labor and capital.

4.2.2 Assumption #2: Exogenous Determination of MFP

There are no diminishing returns to investment in MFP in our model. That means that we are implicitly assuming that firms always use all the technology they can get their hands on! To keep some discipline on the model, we want to restrict the size of MFP and so we assume it is *exogenous*. By exogenous we mean that its level is not determined inside our model; it may change, but we assume that the firm cannot *cause* it to change. Specifically, we will assume that firms cannot invest in patents or other know-how; that innovations just develop exogenously and are not the result of any action taken within our model.

This simplifying assumption is clearly false—firms invest great amounts of money in Research and Development (R & D) in order to improve their production efficiency, and they do this because they expect the return to equal (or exceed!) the cost of that investment. Nonetheless, we define MFP as the contributions to GDP that can *not* be measured by firm Fixed Investment expenditures; all types of Investment that can be measured are contributions to K.

4.2.3 Assumption #3: K Investments Affect GDP with a Lag

We assume that there is a lag between the purchase of a capital good and the impact it has on production. The lag may be short (a day or so for unpacking and installing new software) or quite long (a year or two to build a new factory), depending on the capital good one is considering, but the assumption is that in the aggregate there is on average a delay between the decision to invest in new capital and the period in which the capital gets used. That will have important implications in the model—sometimes firms will find on production day that they have more or less K than they would like, but since it takes time to adjust the capital stock, they are stuck for the time being with what they have. That will imply in our framework that when firms want to make very fast adjustments to production, they will adjust *employment* rather than the capital stock.

This assumption—that short-run movements in GDP will come about because of movements in the Labor input—is well-supported by the data. The level of K tends to move fairly slowly and smoothly (**Figure 2**), whereas the *use* of K (the capacity utilization of capital) moves around a lot. And as we saw in **Chapter 3**, employment moves around a lot as well.

FIGURE 2

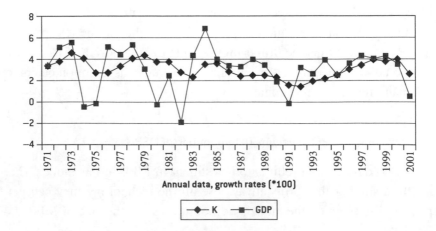

Annual data, growth rates (*100)

AN INTRODUCTION TO MACROECONOMICS

The intuition is that it is easier to cut or add labor shifts than it is to close or open new manufacturing plants, or to sell off or buy new capital equipment, and so last-minute adjustments in production are accommodated by last-minute adjustments in the labor input. In order to build that feature of the economy into the model, we make it impossible to affect current production by changing the current capital stock. The assumption will also make it easier to separate expenditure decisions (buy more capital goods) from production decisions (use more or less of existing capital goods) when we are trying to model the relationship between demand and supply.

4.3 THE LABOR MARKET

4.3.1 The Demand for Labor

Firms demand labor in order to produce output. Under perfect competition, they are willing to pay workers up to the point where their wage is equal to the value of the marginal contribution of their labor input. We know from **Sections 4.1** and **4.2** that the marginal contribution of labor falls as the labor input increases. Thus, holding Prices, K, and MFP constant, firms will only be willing to hire more workers (demand labor) if they are paying a lower wage. We will derive this relationship more carefully in the rest of this section.

First, note that the assumption of diminishing returns gives us a downward-sloping relationship between the marginal productivity of labor (mpl) and L (**Figure 2**).

FIGURE 3

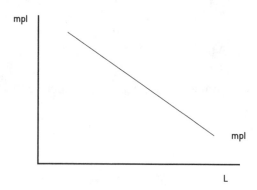

In order to derive a demand curve for labor, we make the additional assumption of perfect competition. Under perfect competition the wage paid (w) is exactly equal to the value of the worker's production, or

$$w = p * mpl$$

where "P" is the aggregate Price level and "w" is an index of aggregate wages.
Rearranging, we have

$$\frac{w}{p} = mpl$$

The term on the left hand side of the equation is known as the "real wage"—it denotes the purchasing power of the nominal wage after *deflating* aggregate wages by the price index. The real wage tells us how many units of GDP worker can buy with their income; in equilibrium, that should be equal to the number of units they've produced as laborers. That is one implication of perfect competition—you get paid what you're worth (to the market!).

We can replace mpl with the "real wage" (nominal wage deflated by the cost of goods and services) on the vertical axis in **Figure 4** to derive the demand curve for labor as a function of the (real) cost of labor. This shows the value of the real wage that firms are willing to pay at any level of employment.

FIGURE 4

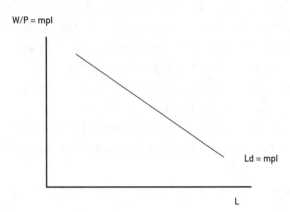

In summary, two assumptions are necessary to derive the demand for labor:

- Diminishing returns

- Perfect competition

4.3.2 The Supply of Labor

Individuals supply labor in order to receive a wage with which they can buy goods and services. Individuals care about the purchasing power of their wage, and so they are concerned about w/p. There is a cost to working, and that cost is the opportunity cost of giving up activities that *don't* earn a market wage.

We assume that the less non-market time an individual has, the more he or she values it and so the more s/he must be paid (in real terms) in order to be willing to work. Graphically, that means that the supply of labor is an increasing function of the real wage (**Figure 5**).

FIGURE 5

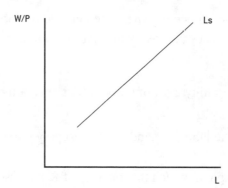

To understand why non-market time becomes more valuable as it becomes more scarce, consider two types of non-market activities: Leisure and Home Production.

4.3.2.1 Leisure

Leisure activities are pure consumption goods from the point of view of the individual—they produce nothing but immediate utility. They include things like sleep, watching television, exercise, and playing with the kids or the dog. We could do those things all day and be happy, but the truth is that after the 12th hour of sleep and the 4th hour of playing with the dog, we aren't gaining much in the way of utility. There are *diminishing returns in utility* to leisure activities. That means that if we have a lot of leisure time, we won't require a very high (real) wage to get us to work a little bit. At the same time, the more sleep and recreation we give up, the more we value it and so the more we insist on getting paid in order to be willing to provide additional hours of work.

4.3.2.2 Home Production

Home production activities are things that have a market counterpart. We can do our own laundry, gardening, housework, and child care, or we can hire someone else to do those things for us. People who are unemployed tend to do these things for themselves—either because they have quit *in order* to do those things or because they have been fired and now find that they prefer to give up some of their own (relatively less valuable) leisure time rather than pay someone else to do those chores. If market wages are very low, then people may choose to supply very little *market* labor—that does not mean that they are not producing anything, but rather that they may be engaged in doing work for themselves in a way that will not appear in our model *or* in our official employment or output data. (Labor rises as people enter the labor force to be in the household service industry, which is now offering a market wage.)

The higher the market wage (in real terms), the more likely stay-at-home workers are to hire somebody else to do that home production for them. Once that activity gets paid a measured market wage, it becomes part of GDP, and the labor supplied to do the activity becomes part of our official employment data.

4.3.3 Labor market equilibrium

Labor market equilibrium occurs where the demand for labor at a certain real wage is equal to the supply of labor at that same real wage. At that point

$$mpl = \frac{w}{p} = \text{Opportunity Cost of working in terms of the utility value of leisure foregone}$$

A shift in either the labor demand or labor supply curve will change the labor market equilibrium.

Consider an example in which the quantity of K increases. If there is more capital available, then the mpl of each worker will increase regardless of how many workers are employed; in other words, the mpl is higher at any level of L. That means that firms will be willing to pay a higher real wage at any level of L. The labor demand curve shows how much firms are willing to pay, and so the increase in K is represented by an upward shift in the Labor demand curve (see **Figure 6**).

To understand how the Labor market moves to a new equilibrium following a shift in one of the curves, you must keep in mind that it is assumed in our model that *perfect competition always holds*. Therefore if mpl increases at L1, then real wages must immediately increase (workers are worth more, and firms must pay them more or they will quit and go work for someone who will). In **Figure 6**, w/p rises to w/p(temp) (straight up from the old equilibrium, on the new Labor demand curve).

FIGURE 6

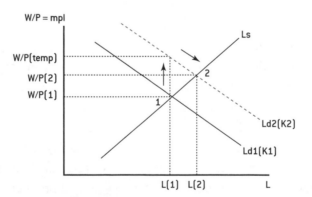

At w/p(temp) Labor supply is greater than Labor demand and firms are able to hire more workers. As L increases, however, the mpl falls (because of diminishing returns) and so, under perfect competition, the real wage offered must also fall (otherwise firms are paying workers more than they are worth, which would mean negative profits for the firm). Graphically, this means that we move down and along the Labor demand curve to an eventual new equilibrium at point 2. At L2, real wages are again equal to the opportunity cost of working in terms of leisure foregone, and there is no longer any incentive for either real wages or employment to change.

It is very important in our model that all Labor market adjustments are movements along the Labor demand curve. Labor demand shows all the points where perfect competition holds, and so we are always on that curve (perfect competition does not affect labor supply—households do not go out of business if they get paid less than the value of their leisure).

4.4   THE CAPITAL MARKET IS THE MARKET FOR LOANS TO FIRMS

Firms invest in capital goods in order to produce output in the future. Imagine that the firm takes money out of savings and buys the capital good this period. Output is produced next period, at which point the firm sells the capital good for the same price it paid for it.

What has the firm gained and lost over the two periods? It pays the capital price but then gets that back the next period. It earns the marginal productivity of capital (mpk), so that is pure gain. On the other hand the firm loses the interest it could have earned if it had left its money in the bank rather than bought the capital good. However, if there was any inflation between the two periods, then the purchasing power of that interest foregone is reduced, and so we want to account for that as well.

In perfect competition, the cost and the benefit of borrowing to get an additional capital good for one period should exactly offset one another—there should be no marginal profit.

In other words, the assumption of perfect competition implies that

$$mpk = \text{interest rate} - \text{inflation} = \text{real interest rate} = r$$

This implies that the cost of capital (return on lending to firms) is the cost of a loan, and so the market for capital is really a market for loans to firms. Households lend to firms in order to earn an interest rate, and firms borrow in order to earn the mpk. In some cases, households are themselves firm-owners (lending to themselves) just as in some cases workers in the labor market are self-employed. In an aggregate model these distinctions about who the players are is unimportant, however.

4.4.1   The Demand for Capital

There are diminishing returns to capital in our model; therefore, holding L and MFP constant, the firm will only demand a marginal unit of capital if the real interest rate is falling enough to offset the fall in mpk. (We will ignore depreciation when talking about the capital market and assume that an increase in new capital also increases the capital stock; in effect we are assuming that the marginal productivity of investment is equal to the marginal productivity of capital.) Capital demand is shown graphically in **Figure 7**.

FIGURE 7

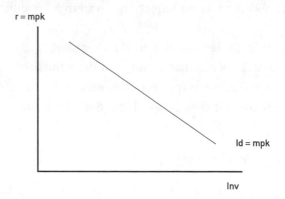

4.4.2 The Supply of Capital

In order to buy capital, firms need savings. They can use their own savings or they can borrow from someone else's savings, but any way you look at it, the financing for new capital comes from somebody's savings. Regardless of where the money comes from, we'll show below that the opportunity cost of using savings to buy a new capital good is the real interest rate.

Consider three ways of financing an Investment:

- The firm uses its own savings, in which case it gives up the interest it could have earned in a bank

- The firm borrows from someone else, in which case the lender is giving up interest that could have been earned in a bank; under perfect competition the firm will pay the lender the same amount the bank will, and so firm must pay the lender an interest rate for the loan

- The firm rents the capital from someone, whose cost is equal to the nominal interest rate because they have financed it either with their own money or a loan; under perfect competition the person renting out the capital can only charge a rate that just covers their costs, and so the rental rate is equal to the interest rate.

In terms of our model, we need to know the relationship between the return to Savings and the quantity of savings in order to graph our Investment Supply curve and so we define the Savings in terms of the utility foregone that could have been earned by Consuming. The opportunity cost of saving of course is less consumption, and people like to consume! Moreover, people get diminishing returns in utility to Consuming, which means that the less they are saving (the higher is Consumption), the lower the real interest rate necessary to satisfy the loan-supply side of the market. Thus, in order to encourage people to lend more money, a higher real interest rate must be offered. The supply of savings to the investment market is shown in **Figure 8**.

FIGURE 8

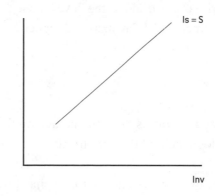

4.4.3   Capital Market Equilibrium

Capital market equilibrium occurs where the demand for investment at a certain real interest rate is equal to the supply of savings at that same real interest rate. At that point

mpk = r = Opportunity Cost of Saving in terms of the utility value of consumption foregone

    A shift in either the demand for Investment or the supply of Savings curve will affect the capital market equilibrium. An increase in MFP or in L will cause the productivity of new capital to rise at any level of Investment, and so the Investment demand curve will shift up, as shown in **Figure 9**. Firms will be willing to pay a higher real interest rate at the old level of I and, under perfect competition, the return earned on loans will rise immediately to r(temp). Savers will be encouraged to increase savings (Investment Supply is greater than Investment Demand at r(temp)) by the higher rate of return.

FIGURE 9

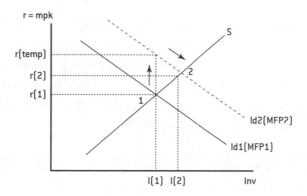

    Just as in the Labor market, the assumption of perfect competition assures that capital market movements take place along the Investment *Demand* curve. As firms are able to buy more

Investments (get more loans at the higher real interest rate), the marginal productivity of each investment falls and we move along the Investment demand curve to a new equilibrium at a higher level of Investment (and Savings) and higher equilibrium real interest rate (point 2).

PRACTICE PROBLEMS

It is often argued that productivity is the ultimate determinant of the standard of living; these questions will illustrate the logic behind that argument.

1. Show the graph for the market for capital Investments. Use your graph to show the impact of a decrease in MFP. Explain how it is that the market for investments will move to a new equilibrium.

2. Show the graph for the market for Labor. Use your graph to show the impact of a decrease in MFP also considering the impact of a decrease in MFP on the capital stock (as shown in Question 1). Explain how it is that the market for labor move to a new equilibrium.

3. Based on your answers to Questions 1 and 2, briefly explain why the impact of a fall in MFP on the capital and labor markets implies a fall in the standard of living.

SUGGESTED ANSWERS

1. The technology used to produce with capital goods is no longer as good as it once was, and so there is less output per input of capital good. Because mpk falls at any level of Investment demand, this is represented as a downward shift in the Investment demand curve to Id2. With the fall in MFP, the marginal productivity of the existing capital stock falls immediately to r(temp) and, under perfect competition, that is exactly the rate of return firms can offer on investments.

At r(temp), households' desired level of Savings is less than actual Savings (equal to Id1), and they threaten to reduce lending if they don't get a higher rate of return. As firms get fewer loans, I falls (move along Id2) and mpk rises (because of diminishing returns to Investment). Under perfect competition, as mpk rises r rises as well. We continue to move along the Id curve until we reach an equilibrium at r2 and I2, with a lower level of Investment and lower equilibrium real interest rates.

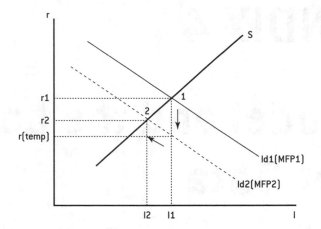

2. Lower MFP implies lower I, which implies a reduction in the capital stock. If both MFP and K are lower, then the marginal productivity of labor is lower at any level of employment, and the labor demand curve shifts down to Ld2. The mpl of the existing workforce falls immediately to w/p(temp) and, under perfect competition, that is exactly the real wage firms can offer to workers.

At w/p(temp), households' desired level of employment is less than actual employment (equal to Ld2), and they threaten to quit if they don't get a higher real wage. As firms employ fewer workers, L falls (move along Ld2) and mpl rises (because of diminishing returns to Labor). Under perfect competition, as mpl rises w/p rises as well. We continue to move along the Ld curve until we reach an equilibrium at w/p2 and L2, with a lower level of Investment and lower equilibrium real wages.

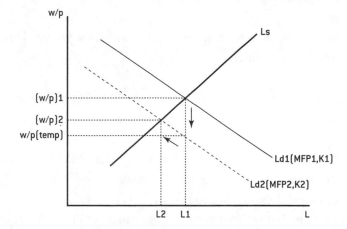

3. A fall in the real wage is a reduction in the amount of goods and services workers can purchase with their earnings, and so it is a fall in their standards of living. The fall in MFP would cause real wages to fall, and standards of living of workers to fall on its own. But the impact of the fall in MFP on the capital market (the other determinant of mpl and thereby real wages), causes real wages to fall even further. Moreover, the purchasing power of capitalist income (the real interest rate) also falls when MFP falls, and so their standards of living are falling as well.

APPENDIX 4

The Model and the Labor Market Data

The model presented in Chapter 4 has two strong implications about the labor market:

- Short-term movements in GDP should be contemporaneous with short-term movements in employment

- There is no unemployment in equilibrium

The first implication is a result of the assumptions about our production function; the second implication is the result of perfect competition.

In the real world:

- GDP rises in the data several months before employment does, and falls several months before employment falls

- There is unemployment in equilibrium—roughly 5% of the labor force is unemployed even when there is no observable market pressure on wages or employment to change.

The *good* news is that there is a much better model of the labor market that can explain those two real-world observations; that model is known as one with "frictions" (for reasons that will be explained in the following Section).

The *bad* news is that we're not going to use that better model in this course! There are three principal reasons for this

- The labor-frictions model doesn't link up as easily to the capital market or goods market models that we will want to integrate into our macroeconomic framework.

- The general business-cycle implications of the simple model we will be using are very similar to what is implied by the labor-frictions model, so we may as well use the easier one!

- The labor-frictions model can yield more than one equilibrium—i.e. supply and demand cross at more than one point. That is manageable (though difficult) if we are using math to talk about economics rather than pictures, but it makes for extremely complex graphing and so it's not very user-friendly in an introductory economics course.

In summary, there mightn't be enough bang-for-the-buck from using the more sophisticated labor model in this text. On the other hand, it will be useful for you to have a general understanding of the model of labor market frictions in order to better understand the employment data.

4A.2   THE MODEL OF FRICTIONS IN THE LABOR MARKET

Labor is a commodity that is supplied by households and for which demand is provided by "firms" even if that worker is self-employed. Even a self-employed worker does not work twenty-four hours a day: there are cost-benefit tradeoffs to working that apply to all worker-firm relationships. Thus the idea of supply and demand in the labor market has some intuitive appeal and to that extent labor markets are like the market for apples or anything else.

Other aspects of the labor market however differ importantly from the mechanics of the market for apples. If a consumer buys an apple one day he or she is under no obligation to do so the next, but that is not generally the case in the labor market—labor contracts often require that a worker receive severance pay upon termination of employment, and the federal government taxes large firms that repeatedly lay off workers as a way of helping to finance unemployment benefits provided by the government. *Firing costs* such as these may make it more expensive to fire a worker than to continue to employ one that isn't needed—these costs are called labor market *frictions* because they keep the labor market from operating as smoothly as implied by perfect competition.

Labor market frictions exist on the hiring side as well. For one thing, firms are hesitant to hire workers because they know how expensive it will be to fire them later on! So, they hesitate to hire new workers during upturns and instead pay their existing workforce overtime to help boost production.

Consider the implication of firing costs for the labor market data: Employment doesn't fall as GDP falls unless *and until* the fall in output is large enough to compensate for firing costs (L falls after GDP falls); at the same time, Employment doesn't rise as GDP rises unless and until firms are convinced the increased demand for labor is here to stay (L rises after GDP rises). This stickiness in the labor market is often referred to as *labor hoarding*: Firms "hoard" workers during downturns so that they may have them during the upturns.

The implications of the labor-friction model are fairly easy to understand, but are not represented by our perfectly competitive model. Other types of labor market frictions include:

- If there are unemployment benefits offered by the government, then workers may choose to stay unemployed rather than accept the first few jobs they find vacant—perhaps because they believe they can find something with higher pay or because there is some non-economic aspect of the jobs they have seen so far that is not as good as what they expect to find if they continue to search. Unemployment benefits prolong search and so they prolong unemployment.

- Even in the absence of unemployment benefits, search frictions imply that there is always some unemployment even when the labor market is in equilibrium: Some people are unemployed by choice because they are searching for something better.

- Training: Firms may incur large training costs for new employees. These hiring costs make firms hesitant to hire new workers. At the same time, if a firm fires a trained worker, it is throwing away the investment it has made in that employee. Thus hiring costs, like firing costs, make firms hesitate to either hire or fire employees.

- Frictions affect real wages as well as equilibrium employment. If it takes time for a firm to fill a vacancy or for a worker to find a job, then there are costs associated with search in terms of income foregone. These costs may make firms and workers hesitate to break their matches even if they know that people at other firms (or employers at other firms) are getting a better deal—that means that identical workers may earn different pay at different jobs! This is very unlike the market for apples, in which the law of one price (perfect competition) is a much more reasonable assumption.

4A.2   MAKING SENSE OF LABOR MARKET DATA

Chapter 4 presents a model of the labor market that implies that employment will rise (and unemployment will fall) as GDP rises; that is not what we see in the data. The labor-frictions model implies that employment movements will lag GDP movements; that is what we see in the data and so that is some support for the labor-frictions model.

Secondly, the model in Chapter 4 implies that in equilibrium all workers that want jobs at the market wage will have jobs; that is not what we see in the data. The labor-frictions model, on the other hand, implies that some workers will be searching for jobs even when the labor market is in equilibrium.

What's more, labor hoarding of the kind predicted by the labor-frictions model will cause labor productivity to rise as GDP rises and fall as GDP falls, and that is something else that we see in the data. On the other hand, our model also tells us that if MFP rises or falls then it will cause GDP to rise or fall. Consequently it is hard to tell if productivity moves with GDP over the cycle because it is *causing* the cycle or because there is labor hoarding.

HONORS APPENDIX 4

Mathematical Derivation of Labor and Capital Demand Curves

4B.1   A COBB-DOUGLAS PRODUCTION FUNCTION

Consider the following production function for the aggregate economy:

$$GDP = f(MFP, L, K) = MFP \cdot L^{\frac{1}{3}} \cdot K^{\frac{2}{3}}$$

where GDP is a function of three variables: Multifactor Productivity (MFP), Labor (L), and Capital (K). There are exponential weights on each input (the weight on MFP is equal to one). This is known as a Cobb-Douglas production function, and it is a form commonly used in macroeconomic modeling.

In this example, the derivatives of GDP with respect to L or K have economic interpretations:

- f ′(L) = the marginal contribution of L to GDP
  - ○ *f ′(L) is the marginal productivity of labor*
  - ○ $f'(L) = \dfrac{1}{3} \cdot MFP \cdot L^{\frac{-2}{3}} \cdot K^{\frac{2}{3}}$
  - ○ $f'(L) = \dfrac{1}{3} \cdot MFP \cdot L^{\frac{1}{3}} \cdot L^{-1} \cdot K^{\frac{2}{3}}$
  - ○ $f'(K) = \dfrac{1}{3} \cdot \dfrac{GDP}{L} > 0$

- f ′(K) = the marginal contribution of K to GDP
  - ○ *f ′(K) is the marginal productivity of capital*
  - ○ $f'(K) = \dfrac{2}{3} \cdot MFP \cdot L^{\frac{1}{3}} \cdot K^{-\frac{1}{3}}$

o $f'(K) = \dfrac{2}{3} \cdot MFP \cdot L^{\frac{1}{3}} \cdot K^{\frac{2}{3}} \cdot K^{-1}$

o $f'(D) = \dfrac{2}{3} \cdot \dfrac{GDP}{K} > 0$

The Assumption of Diminishing Returns in Production

The assumption of diminishing returns implies that the marginal productivity of the input falls as the quantity of the input increases. The mathematical equivalent of that statement is that the derivative of the marginal product with respect to the input is less than zero. It can be shown that the production function in **Section 4A.1** has diminishing returns to both the capital and the labor inputs:

The marginal productivity of labor is defined as

$$mpl = g(L) = \frac{1}{3} \cdot \frac{GDP}{L} = \frac{1}{3} \cdot MFP \cdot L^{-\frac{2}{3}} \cdot K^{\frac{2}{3}}$$

The derivative of mpl with respect to L is

$$g'(L) = \frac{1}{3} \cdot \left(\frac{-2}{3}\right) \cdot MFP \cdot L^{\frac{-5}{3}} \cdot K^{\frac{2}{3}} < 0$$

It is easy to show that the derivative of mpk with respect to K is also negative.

Graphically, that means that if we plot mpl (mpk) as a function of L (K), that the marginal productivity has a negative slope—in other words, marginal productivity falls as the input rises. Adding the assumption of perfect competition allows us to derive downward sloping demand curves as in **Figures 4 and 7** in Chapter 4 of the text.

As we have just seen, that assumption of diminishing returns to any input is actually a mathematical restriction on the marginal contributions of the inputs into the production function. That mathematical restriction is that the derivative of the marginal productivity (the derivative of the derivative) must be less than zero. Statistical methods used to try to estimate the coefficients on aggregate production function indicate these are reasonable (though still not uncontroversial) assumptions.

Shifts in the Labor and Capital Demand Curves

Consider again the equation that defines labor demand in our hypothetical production function:

$$w/p = mpl = g(MFP,K,L) = \frac{1}{3} \cdot \frac{GDP}{L} = \frac{1}{3} \cdot MFP \cdot L^{-\frac{2}{3}} \cdot K^{\frac{2}{3}}$$

We've shown that mpl falls as the labor input rises, but factors other than L also affect the marginal productivity of labor: MFP and K.

Consider for example the impact of an increase in MFP on labor demand:

$$g'(\text{MFP}) = \frac{1}{3} \cdot 1 \cdot \text{MFP}^0 \cdot L^{\frac{-2}{3}} \cdot K^{\frac{2}{3}} = \frac{1}{3} \cdot L^{\frac{-2}{3}} \cdot K^{\frac{2}{3}} > 0$$

Holding L constant, mpl increases with increases in MFP (the derivative of mpl with respect to MFP is positive). It is easy to show that this is also true for any marginal change in K.

Graphically, that means that the labor demand curve shifts up (higher at any level of L) when MPF or K increase, and shifts down (lower at any level of L) when MFP or K decrease. The derivative with the object not on the axis *shifts* the curve, and the numbers on the production function determine how much the curve shifts.

Symmetric arguments can be made for the capital demand curve; the derivative of mpk with respect to the capital stock determines the slope of the curve, the derivative of mpk with respect to the other inputs determines shifts in the investment demand curve.

ECONOMIC GROWTH

Output growth requires input growth. In the terminology of the production function defined in **Chapter 4**, GDP growth is the result of growth in MFP, L, or K. We have assumed that MFP growth is exogenous, but what determines growth in each of the other inputs?

5.1   EMPLOYMENT GROWTH

The supply of labor is bounded by the total available labor force; even at infinitely large labor demand (infinitely large real wages), employment growth is limited by population growth. We will assume that population growth is exogenous, which means that we will not be able to explain it with our model. Instead, we will usually use our model to understand how labor market equilibrium is affected by changes in MFP and K (things that shift the Labor *demand* curve). Nonetheless, economic growth will be affected by growth in any of the three inputs into production, and so in the remainder of this Section we will briefly discuss the impact of population growth on our model.

5.1.1   Is Population Growth Good for the Economy?

Two hundred years ago, Thomas Malthus used economic theory to predict that unless public measures were taken to halt rapid increases in population growth, standards of living would fall to dangerously low levels. The argument was based on an economic model quite like the one we have developed: If there are more workers then, all other things being equal, diminishing returns to labor will kick in and output per person (standards of living) will fall. Because of these predictions, economics came to be known (somewhat sarcastically!) as the "dismal science".

Malthus' dismal forecast was wrong, of course, and for two reasons. First, population growth (Labor Supply shifts) did not procede as quickly as Malthus forecast. Second, gains in MFP (Labor Demand shifts) put upward pressure on labor productivity—so much so that it more than offset the diminishing returns influence of population growth.

Although it is important for real wage growth that the influences of increases in labor demand outstrip labor supply, there are also some costs to modern economies of slowing population growth. Consider for example the U.S. Social Security and Medicare programs that support the elderly—those systems are paid for by the tax contributions of the young: The fewer young people we have (due to slower population growth), the more difficult it will be to pay for those programs for the elderly.

FIGURE 1

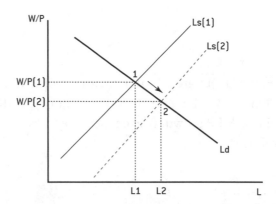

5.1.2 Income and Substitution Effects in Labor Supply

The second potential source of employment growth is that increased labor productivity may encourage workers to give up more leisure time as shifts in Labor Demand may cause equilibrium employment to increase as we move along an upward-sloping Labor Supply curve (see **Chapter 4, Figure 6**). As MFP increases, both K and L increase *endogenously* (as a result of the MFP increase) and so in the end MFP contributions threefold to GDP growth.

It turns out, however, that *labor force participation rates* (the labor force as a share of the working age population) and average hourly workweeks have not changed significantly in the last 50 years despite rapid productivity gains. This suggests that although rising real wages may be encouraging workers to substitute away from leisure into employment, that there is an offsetting effect on Labor Supply: That effect is known as the *income effect*. Increases in income allow workers to increase both their leisure and their consumption at the same time because they can work fewer hours at a higher real wage. The income effect causes labor supply to *fall* as real wages increase.

In the U.S. data, it seems that these income and substitution effects in labor supply have roughly cancelled each other over the last 50 years so that individual labor supply has been roughly unaffected as real wages have increased. In terms of our graphical analysis, this hypothetical income effect at high real wages would be demonstrated by a labor supply curve that is roughly vertical over the range of real wages we've seen in recent years in the U.S., and may even be backward-bending at very high levels of the real wage where the income effect dominates the substitution effect (**Figure 2**).

Of course, the labor force participation rate does move in response to real wages in the way described in **Chapter 4**, but it only does so on a temporary basis; on average, the fraction of males working and the number of hours worked per week stays fairly constant over time.[1]

FIGURE 2

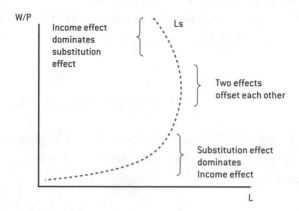

5.2   CAPITAL STOCK GROWTH

Whereas MFP and Population growth are exogenous to (determined outside of) the model, the level of capital growth is determined entirely within the model framework. In other words, the source of capital growth are changes in either of those other factors (changes in MFP or in population growth). To why this is so, consider that the amount of savings available for investment loans is determined by income growth—how much can be saved depends on how much can be earned—and so Savings is not the *source* of income growth. At the same time, demand for capital depends on its productivity, which will be determined by the amount of labor available (population growth) and on the technology available to make use of the capital and labor inputs (MFP).

To summarize: The only determinants of economic growth are changes in population and changes in MFP.

5.3   ESTIMATING MFP

MFP is an input that affects the productivity of all capital and labor inputs equally. Examples include technological innovations that allow us to use our existing labor and capital more efficiently (like how to make stronger steel), managerial practices that keep resources from being wasted (like better inventory management or double-entry bookkeeping), the ability to use the most efficient production method (like electricity or irrigation), and so on.

---

[1]Female labor force participation rates increased steadily over the 20th century, but the data suggest that this trend may be leveling off.

In general, MFP consists of a huge variety of inputs into production, all of which involve know-how or experience, and most of which are unobservable! We do not have any direct observations of MFP for any industry, and if we did, it is not clear how we might put values on those bits of knowledge in order to create an aggregate MFP measure.

Robert Solow, a Nobel Prize winning economist, suggested instead that we measure MFP as a *residual* of things for which we *do* have data.

Working with our sample production function, we can attribute GDP growth to growth in the three inputs, assuming that the function f that determines their contribution to GDP doesn't change over time:

$$\dot{GDP} = \dot{MFP} + f_L(\dot{L}) + f_K(\dot{K})$$

where fL and fK measure the contribution of L and K growth to GDP growth. Rearranging terms, we can estimate MFP growth as the residual of output growth net of the contribution of its observable inputs:

$$\dot{MFP} = \dot{GDP} - f_L(\dot{L}) - f_K(\dot{K})$$

The accuracy of this residual measure of productivity is not without controversy. There are potentially as many estimates of MFP growth as there are models of the production function! Moreover, GDP, Labor and the Capital stock data are all imperfectly measured, which means that the MFP estimate incorporates the measurement error of all three of those pieces of data.

We have many data measurement problems in macreconomics, but measurement or potential *mis*-measurement of MFP is particularly frustrating to economists because of its importance—it is the ultimate determinant of standards of living and yet it is unobservable.

5.4   POLICIES THAT SUPPORT ECONOMIC GROWTH

We assume in our model that MFP growth is exogenous, which implies that there is no market for it (it is determined outside our modeling framework). We make that assumption because there is no direct link between money spent trying to develop ideas and the returns to those investments. MFP depends on investments in new ideas, to be sure, but it also seems to be determined to a great extent by sheer luck! In our model we assume that "luck" (an exogenous variable) is the primary determinant of MFP growth, but a few of the other influences are described in the rest of this section.

5.4.1   Support of Research and Development

In our framework, technological progress is unaffected by firm or government action. In reality, firms do engage in research and development in order to develop new products; the cost is sometimes extremely high—it may take years of investment before there is a marketable innovation, or there may be no profitable outcome at all. In order to encourage firms to engage in such risky activities, governments provide systems of property right protection and patent laws, so that firms that do make successful innovations will, at least for a short time, reap sufficient profits that they can pay off their debts. That is one way of raising the *benefits* of Research and Development.

Methods of reducing the *costs* of research and development include competitive government research grants, tax deductions for research expenditures, and of course education subsidies through public schooling and student loans.

Also, support of a competitive marketplace also encourages product innovation because it is necessary in order to keep up with other firms that are engaging in such activity.

5.4.2 Well-functioning Financial Markets

An increase in MFP directly causes GDP to increase; it also *indirectly* causes GDP to increase if the increased demand for capital results in a higher capital stock. Capital productivity and therefore capital demand certainly rises as MFP rises, but the increase in equilibrium capital requires that financial markets are working well enough to allocate savings to firms. We'll return to this issue several times in later chapters of the text.

PRACTICE PROBLEMS

1. Graph the market for labor assuming the labor market is in equilibrium and that labor supply is upward-sloping. Explain the impact of an increase in MFP on the market for labor, making sure to explain why the economy moves toward equilibrium in the way you indicate in your graph

2. Using your graph from Question 1, show why it is that if population growth exceeds productivity growth, we will get declining real wages. Describe the market forces that cause the economy to move to this new equilibrium.

SUGGESTED ANSWERS

1. If MFP increases, then the marginal productivity of labor (mpl) increases at any level of employment, and the labor demand curve shifts up (firms are willing to pay a higher real wage at any level of employment). As MFP increases, mpl increases at the original equilibrium level of employment, and so under perfect competition real wages immediately rise to w/p(temp). At that high real wage, the amount workers want to work exceeds actual employment, and so firms are able to hire more workers. As L increases, mpl falls because of diminishing returns, and so under perfect competition real wages fall as well as we move along the labor demand curve to a new equilibrium with higher real wages than where we started and a higher level of employment.

2. As population grows, there are more workers at any real wage and the labor supply curve shifts to the right. There is no change in mpl and so no immediate change in real wages at the origi-

nal level of employment, but at that initial real wage the amount workers want to work exceeds actual employment, and so firms are able to hire more workers. As L increases, mpl falls because of diminishing returns, and so under perfect competition real wages fall as well as we move along the labor demand curve to a new equilibrium with higher real wages than where we started and a higher level of employment.

If the shift in the labor supply curve (population growth) is sufficiently large relatively to the shift in labor demand (productivity growth), then real wages will fall and standards of living will fall.

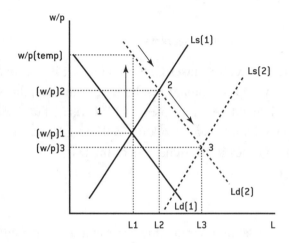

APPENDIX 5

The Model
and the MFP Data

Section 5.3 presents the most common means of estimating MFP growth, which is as a residual of GDP and its observable inputs. We have no way of directly observing if this estimate is correct, because MFP is by definition unobservable. Moreover, efforts to *indirectly* estimate changes in MFP have not been a great success: Economists find little correlation between measured MFP growth and the number of new patents on file, for example, largely because most new patents are never used in the production of goods and services. What's more, is no reliable relationship between Research and Development expenditures by firms and measured MFP growth, in part because of long lags between the point at which research begins and when the research bears economic fruit, but also because so much research and development expenditure is, in the end, economically unprofitable.

Although there is no better way to measure MFP other than as a residual of GDP and its observable inputs, there are two important flaws with its estimation:

1. In order to calculate MFP, the economist must make assumptions about industry production functions; those assumptions are by necessity simplistic and are probably only correct on average for each industry (if they are correct at all!) but may not good approximations of firm-level technologies.
2. Even if the production function assumed is a good approximation, the labor, capital, and GDP data used to estimate MFP are flawed, and so the MFP estimate inherits those flaws.

LABOR MARKET FRICTIONS AND THE MFP ESTIMATE

The **Chapter 4 Appendix** discusses an alternative model of the aggregate labor market in which frictions keep employment from moving the way implied by the perfectly competitive model assumed in this text. Because MFP is measured as a residual, any mis-measurement of the contribution of L that may result from *labor-hoarding*, will result in mis-measurement of MFP.

Assume that we observe GDP fall, no change in the capital stock, and no change in employment. Assume further that there is labor hoarding. Remember that labor hoarding implies that the *use* of workers will rise and fall with changes in GDP, but that the *employment* of workers will not (or not immediately, at any rate). Thus it is quite likely that some of the GDP decrease is the result of MFP decreasing, and the rest the result of an *endogenous* decrease in the labor input (as MFP falls, firms demand less of their existing workforce).

Our model however does not take labor hoarding into consideration—in our model, *all* of the decrease in GDP would be measured as the result of a change in the unobservable input: MFP. In this case, we'd overestimate the decrease in MFP.

In general, labor hoarding, if it exists, causes us to over-estimate MFP when GDP is increasing and to under-estimate MFP when GDP is falling. Consequently, it may look as though MFP is much more important in determining GDP than it actually is!

MULTIPLE DATA ERRORS IN ESTIMATING MFP

There are errors in estimating GDP, K, and L. MFP is the residual of those estimates, and so the MFP estimate reflects errors in estimating each of those pieces of data.

Moreover, MFP is measured as the residual of GDP and the *observable* inputs. The U.S. occasionally changes what is observable, which means that it is occasionally changing what MFP *means*. So, for example, U.S. government statistics recently began including internal (firm-specific) software development in its estimate of the domestic capital stock: Changing the way that the capital stock was measured caused a large upward-revision to our capital estimates for the 1990s, and to a consequent downward-revision to our MFP estimate for the same period! The "new economy" period is now less often described as a "high productivity" period, and more often referred to as a period of tremendous "capital deepening" (increases in the quality and/or quantity of the capital stock).

THE BUSINESS CYCLE

Chapter 5 introduced us to the causes of economic growth. While we know that the trend, or average, rate of growth varies over time, we also know that the economy tends to wiggle around trend increases in growth. The 1990s, for example, were a period of relatively strong growth, reflected in a bigger trend growth rate, but some quarters and years were stronger than others. This chapter introduces the concept of the business cycle—the movements around trend economic growth.

6.1   TRENDS AND CYCLES IN ECONOMIC DATA

Figure 1 plots U.S. real GDP, after taking logs of the time series (a time series is a series of data points over time). Economic data are often presented in log format because the slope of a log variable (the rise over the run) approximates the growth rate. If the plot in **Figure 1** is steeper in some years than in others, that means that the growth rate of GDP is higher in those years. Close inspection of the graph reveals that U.S. GDP hasn't grown at a steady pace: There are long periods of slow growth and long periods of faster growth.

Trend GDP is shown as the bold line in **Figure 2**. It looks as though we have just drawn a smooth line through the middle of the scattered GDP points, but in fact a statistical method was used to estimate that trend; that method calculates a moving (or changing) average over time—the trend is just the average.

Logically, cyclical movements in output must result from cyclical movements in the inputs into the production function; Employment (**Figure 3**) also has an upward trend, with cycles highly correlated with those for GDP.

It should be clear that not all of the time series' movement can be explained by the trend; temporary factors also affect GDP and its inputs. These "deviations from trend" are referred to as *cyclical* movements in the data because, by definition, a fall below trend in one period implies that the data will rise above trend in another period. A de-trended piece of data is just the actual data minus the trend. **Figures 4a-d** presents de-trended time series data for GDP, MFP, K, and L.

FIGURE 1: LOG GDP (INDEX: GDP = 100 IN 2000)

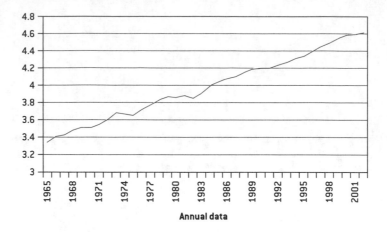

FIGURE 2:LOG GDP AND TREND GDP (INDEX: GDP = 100 IN 2000)

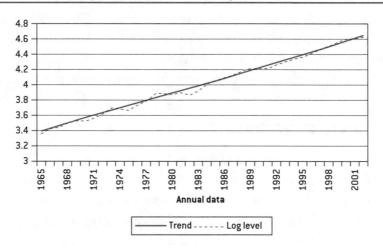

FIGURE 3:LOG L AND TREND L (INDEX: L=100 IN 2000)

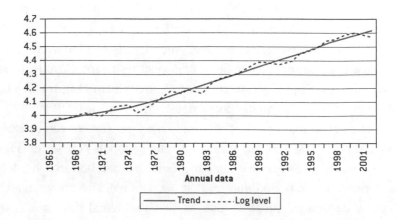

FIGURE 4A: CYCLE IN GDP

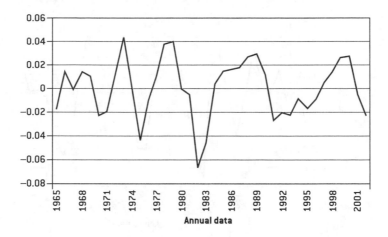

FIGURE 4B: CYCLE IN MFP

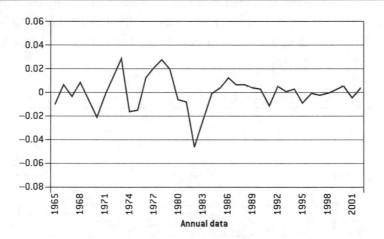

FIGURE 4C: CYCLE IN K INPUT

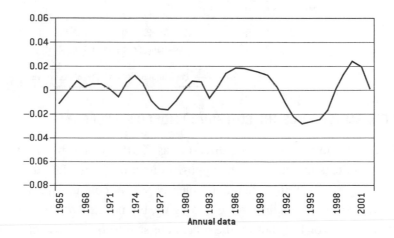

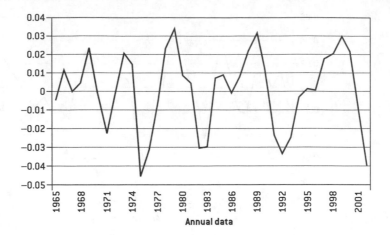

Annual data

Figure 5 presents de-trended log time series data for two Aggregate Expenditure components of GDP: Personal Consumption Expenditures and Private Fixed Investment. If you look closely, you'll see that the cyclical movements in all of these series in **Figures 4 and 5** are clearly related to each other, and so economists refer to their cyclical patterns as all relating to one common "business cycle".

FIGURE 5: CYCLICAL MOVEMENTS IN C AND FIXED I

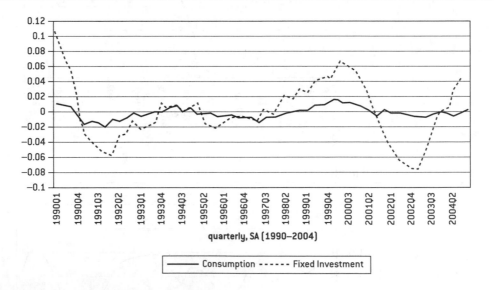

quarterly, SA (1990–2004)

——— Consumption ------ Fixed Investment

6.2   WHAT CHARACTERISTICS ARE COMMON TO MOST U.S. CYCLES?

Variables that move in the same direction as GDP over the business cycle are known as *pro-cyclical*; variables that move in the opposite direction from GDP are known as *counter-cyclical*. And the last group—things that aren't clearly pro- or counter-cyclical— are *acyclic* variables.

Cyclical variables tend to move at roughly, but not *exactly* the same time as GDP. Variables that start to rise (or fall) before the others are said to *lead* the cycle—these *leading indicators* are paid close attention by analysts for that reason, as they can be early warnings of future swings in the economy. Variables that *lag* the cycle—*lagging indicators*—are ones that are affected last by economic disturbances.

Some "stylized facts" (things that are roughly, but not always, true) about U.S. business cycles are:

1. Business Fixed Investment spending is pro-cyclical
2. Business Fixed Investment spending swings more than GDP over the cycle
3. Total Consumption spending is pro-cyclical
4. Total Consumption spending doesn't move as much over the cycle as does GDP
5. Consumption spending on *durable* goods (refrigerators, cars, and so on) leads the cycle
6. Employment is pro-cyclical
7. Employment lags the cycle
8. Measured MFP is pro-cyclical
9. Measured Unemployment often improves mid-cycle as people exit the labor force
10. The Capital Stock moves much less than GDP, L, or MFP over the cycle[1]
11. The Index of Industrial Production is pro-cyclical
12. The value of the stock market is a-cyclical

These stylized facts are interesting to economists! They raise a host of questions about how the market works, such as

- Why is Consumption spending smoother than GDP?

- Why does a crash in the stock market not always relate to a general fall in economic activity?

- Why does spending on things that last a long time (business fixed investment and consumption spending on durables) move differently over the cycle than does spending on other stuff?

- Why is measured MFP pro-cyclical? Is it because business cycles are just part of the process of technological advance, or is it because MFP is mis-measured?

6.3 WHAT'S A RECESSION AND HOW DO WE KNOW IF WE'RE IN ONE?

The word "recession" is used to describe a period of weak economic activity and is usually defined in one of two ways:

---

[1]Points 2 and 10 are not inconsistent—the flow of Investment into the total Capital Stock is relatively small.

A purely statistical description

- An economic variable is in recession if it declines for two consecutive quarters

Or an economic description

- An economic variable is in recession if the level is below trend (the cyclical component is negative)

The second description of recession has more economic meaning: If the economy is growing 1% a year but MFP and the labor force together contribute 3% GDP growth a year, we are growing at a rate below potential and so we know that something is keeping the economy away from its long-run equilibrium growth path—something is *wrong*. Unfortunately, it is hard to know in real time what the trend *is:* MFP is not observable, and can only be estimated once annual capital stock data are collected, and labor force participation falls during downturns, so it is hard to know its trend until the recession is over.

6.3.1 The National Bureau of Economic Research Business Cycle Dating Committee

Because it is difficult to know the current trend, and because we know that current data will be revised at a later date, one method of identifying the stage of the business cycle is to look at a broad set of economic data. If the data are all getting "worse", in some subjective sense, then it is unlikely that any GDP release or data revision is going to change that general impression. And of course if all the data are showing signs of improvement, then the economy is probably doing better. This is not a very scientific method of identifying the stage of the business cycle! However, if you trust the analysts who are looking at the data, you are likely to trust their general sense of things. The National Bureau of Economic Research (NBER) includes a group of academic economists who use their judgment to semi-officially define the state of the U.S. economy in any time period.

The NBER looks at a broad set of data to make its evaluation of the current state of the economy. Because many of the data are available at a monthly frequency, the evaluation can in principle be fairly timely. However, these monthly data are often subject to significant revisions, and so the NBER will often delay several months before announcing a new official business-cycle turning point. Although the Dating Committee will of course consider other factors, the main data that they use as their business cycle indicators are

- GDP

- Employment

- Wholesale and Retail Trade

- Industrial Production

- Personal Income

The NBER Business Cycle Dating Committee envisions the *whole economy* as moving on a wave of activity that rises from some trough or low-point until it reaches a peak, and then contracts to a new trough, expands again, and so on.

- *An NBER-contraction is the period between a peak and a trough.* During an NBER-contraction the economy can still be growing, but be growing by less than it did at the peak.

- *An NBER expansion is the period between a trough and a peak*; during an NBER expansion the economy may still be in decline, but the NBER is labeling it as part of an expansion because it thinks the worst of it is over, and that things are in recovery.

In some sense, the identification of turning points by the NBER is designed to help out those people who haven't the time or ability to look at the data themselves—all the data used by the NBER are public information! However, the NBER report is a useful reference if one is trying to convey a sense of the current economic situation, and so it is often cited by politicians and economic analysts that want an authoritative characterization of the state of the economy.

6.4   WHY DO WE CARE SO MUCH ABOUT BUSINESS CYCLES?

Figure 2 shows the relative magnitude of the cyclical component of real GDP—it is the gap between GDP and the trend line. As you can see, the cycle is quite small compared to total GDP. When presented that way, recessions do not seem to be such a big deal—especially when one considers that they are offset by years of unusually high growth during which people could put aside extra savings to have in reserve for an economic "rainy day".

In reality, however, recessions are not shared equally across members of society; we do not all experience a cut in income or in hours worked that is proportional to the national fall in GDP. Instead, some of us may be barely affected by a particular recession, whereas for others the recession can be economically (and personally) devastating.

Moreover, some occupational groups are more susceptible to high unemployment rates during recessions than are others, which also means that different regions of the U.S. are more strongly impacted by the recession than others; that is because different regions specialize in the production of different types of goods.

Table 1 shows unemployment rates by occupation in 2003 (a year of below-trend employment) using household survey data collected by the Bureau of Labor Statistics. The pattern in **Table 1** is not unusual for U.S. downturns: White-collar workers (management and professional workers) generally have unemployment rates far below the average for the U.S., whereas blue collar workers (in manufacturing production, transportation industries, food preparation, and so on) have unemployment rates that are often far above the U.S average.

TABLE 1: UNEMPLOYMENT RATES BY OCCUPATION, 2003	
Total, 16 years and over	6.0%
Management, Professional, and Related Occupations	3.1%
Service Occupations	7.1%
Sales and Office Occupations	5.5%
Natural Resources, Construction, and Maintenance Occupations	8.1%
Production, Transportation, and material Moving Occupations	7.9%
Source: Bureau of Labor Statistics	

Finally, although it is beyond the scope of our model, we care about recessions because it is possible that cyclical movements may affect trend GDP growth for many years to come. If for example MFP growth is affected by firm investment in Research and Development, then hard times that cause firms to scale back on R&D expenditures may cause a delay in technological progress, which implies lower capital stocks and lower demand for workers in future periods.

Moreover, if worker skills and the contribution of labor are related to their past job experience, then prolonged periods of unemployment will lower future labor productivity by those workers. Longer recessions mean longer periods of skill depreciation; by the second quarter of 2003, the average unemployment duration was nearly 19 weeks, and about 12 percent of those unemployed had been out of work for more than a full year. When a firm is considering hiring a new worker, they may be hesitant to hire someone who has been among the long-term unemployed because those workers have no experience with technologies introduced during their absence, they may forgotten some of the skills they did have, and/or they may have developed bad work habits after having been idle for so long; in each case, the firm is concerned that the productivity of the worker will be low. From the perspective of the worker, long-term unemployment can have a long-term impact on the type of work or salary she or he can earn in the future, and so there are long-term income distributional and societal implications of business cycles.

From the perspective of the macro-economist, the associated potential loss of "human capital" implies lower GDP growth unless or until that worker can be reeducated.

PRACTICE PROBLEMS

1. Go to www.nber.org and follow the links to see their latest report on the current state of the business cycle. Do they identify the economy as currently being in an expansion or a contraction? Why? Is there any inconsistency among the pieces of data that they consider that they feel is making current identification of the stage of the business cycle particularly difficult?

FINANCIAL MARKETS

All Investments are financed (paid for) with someone's savings—either the savings of the capitalist his or herself or by borrowing somebody else's savings in order to pay for the capital good. A financial market is a mechanism through which savings gets allocated to borrowers, and through which borrowers repay lenders. In order to understand the market for capital, then, we have to understand something about how financial markets work to get money to firms so that they can invest in new capital goods. We say that a financial market is one in which *financial assets* are bought and sold; we call loans to firms *assets* because they are claims on future consumption goods and because they represent a *contribution* to overall wealth.

7.1 INTRODUCTION TO FINANCIAL ASSETS

Financial assets include cash as well as loans to other borrowers, because from the lender's perspective those loans are claims on cash in the future. Yearly changes in personal savings, as well as variations in the rate of return earned on those savings, jointly determine the household's stock of financial assets.

Annual contributions to personal savings can be positive (consumption expenditures are less than current after-tax income) or negative (expenditures are greater than current after-tax income), and so the stock of a household's financial assets may rise or fall in a given year. Moreover, a household's stock of financial assets tends to follow predictable patterns over the life cycle; retired people, for example, have negative savings (they are *dis-saving*) and their stock of financial assets is falling as a result.

In our model, households can hold any of four types of financial assets: They can

1. Put it in a bank and earn the deposit or savings account rate
2. Make loans directly to firms and households
3. Buy bonds from firms or governments
4. Buy stocks

The expected return on any one of those types of savings must be the same as any other. Otherwise, people would only allocate their savings to the method that offered the highest return. More savings means more investment, and so under diminishing returns we know the increased demand for the asset with the highest rate of return would drive down its marginal productivity; under prefect competition that also means that increased demand for the asset will drive down its rate of return. The result in equilibrium is that all *expected* returns will be the same.

It is important to keep in mind that it is only the *expected* return that must be equalized across asset types. All other things being equal, the more risk there is, the lower the expectation that the loan will be repaid, and so the loan rate offered will be higher to compensate for that risk.

7.1.1 Checking and Savings Deposits

Banks will offer a fixed interest rate on checking and savings deposits at their institutions; this *deposit rate* is offered to encourage households to lend their money to the bank. Banks can only afford to offer an interest payment on deposits because the banks in turn earn revenue using the deposits to make loans to firms, households, and governments; the rate charged for a loan made by a bank is the *lending rate*.

The *lending-deposit rate spread,* or gap between the rate the bank earns and the interest rate it pays, is the return to the bank for providing the financial service. Under perfect competition, that return will be just high enough to cover the bank's costs.

The more efficient banks are, the lower lending rates are, and the higher the level of Investment as we move down and along an Investment demand curve. Bank costs depend on factors such as

- Credit assessment (collecting the borrower's credit history, forecasting the future ability to repay, profiling the borrower based on age, industry, education, etc)

- Loan Assessment (depending on type of loan: industry expertise and prediction of MPK, housing market forecast, collateral for consumer loans)

- Monitoring (sending out payment reminders, repossessing property, legal action in case of default)

- Risk (the bank absorbs all the risk that the loan may not be paid back)

- The rate banks pay to borrow savings (the deposit rate if they are borrowing from households, the "inter-bank rate" if they are borrowing from other banks, and the cost of bonds or stocks the bank may sell to raise financing)

A temporary change in the lending-deposit spread usually reflects a change in banks' perceptions of risk. An increase in the spread, for example, may result from an increase in uncertainty about the MFP (and therefore mpk) forecast, or it may result from a sense that households and firms are "over-extended" and are trying to borrow more than they can repay, or it may result from increased uncertainty about inflation, and so on.

7.1.2 Lending to Firms and Households

Households may bypass the banking system and lend directly to firms and to each other, thus earning the lending rate rather than the (lower) deposit rate. If households do that, however, they also incur the same intermediation costs that the bank would. Banks are generally more efficient than private households when it comes to intermediation costs, and so it is not generally profitable for most households to make these types of loans themselves.

If the lender and the borrower have a personal history, then of course it possible for intermediation costs to be lower for the lender than for the bank. Corporations often re-invest their earnings into their own firms, for example (these would be corporate profits, which is part of aggregate household income). Households also often use their own savings (or a mix of their own savings and a bank loan) to invest in housing: These households are lending to themselves rather than earning a market return elsewhere.

When banking systems collapse, economies resort to this type of credit market, and so this type of lending is prevalent in many developing countries. It is inefficient however because individuals do not have the expertise in financial intermediation to keep lending rates low, and so the equilibrium capital stock is lower as well.

7.1.3 Company and Government Bonds

A second way that savers and banks make loans is through the purchase of bonds. A bond is a contractual obligation to pay the lender a fixed payment (called a coupon) over a fixed time period, and then to give the lender a certain amount of money back at the end of the loan period. It sounds just like a regular loan, and in many ways it is, but there are some important differences, and a whole lot of terminology! Bonds are generally sold by large corporations and by various levels of government (local, state, national, or international organizations like the World Bank).

Imagine that an individual (household or bank) buys a bond for $1000 that will pay interest of 3% per year for 10 years, after which the borrower will repay the $1000. That describes a bond that is selling at "par"—the price paid is equal to the amount that gets paid back—with a *maturity* of 10 years, and a *coupon* of 3%. The rate of return on the bond is 3% per year, but the total yield to maturity (return over the ten years until maturation of the bond) is 30% (three percent for ten years).

What makes a bond different from a regular loan is that the bond can be sold at any time at any price. Because the yield to maturity is $300, if the 3% coupon looks attractive enough, another saver may be willing to buy the bond from the household for *more* than the $1000 originally paid—anything up to $1300.

As the price of the bond changes, the *yield*, or return on the bond, changes as well. The secondary market (resale market) price of the bond can rise anywhere up to $1300 or even all the way down to zero if the likelihood of meeting the loan obligation falls low enough. All other things being equal, the higher the price paid, the lower the rate of return.

To summarize what we've got so far: Bonds offer a *fixed income* in terms of their return, because the coupon rate paid and the amount paid at maturity are never renegotiated. The price of the bond may vary over time as people who own bonds re-sell them to other people (because they need money to buy goods and services, or because they want to do something else with their savings). As the price of the bond rises, the yield falls.

There are essentially two factors that cause secondary bond prices to move: inflation and risk. First, there is some risk that the borrower may default on the bond, paying less than all of the coupon promised and/or less than all of the maturity payment promised. That risk is incorporated into the original price and coupon on the bond, but that risk may change before the bond matures. Agencies that rate bond debt (like Moody's or Standard and Poor's) rank the quality of a company's or a government's bonds. The highest rating is for *investment grade* bonds (Aaa, Aa, etc down to Ba) and the lowest rating is for what are called *junk bonds* (Bb and further down the alphabet). The quality rating is a signal to financial market participants; junk bonds offer high coupon rates to compensate for their risk, and if either junk or investment-grade bonds become riskier once they've initially be sold then they will trade at low prices in secondary markets in order to compensate buyers and improve the expected yield.

The second factor that causes bond prices to move is inflationary expectations. Inflation eats away at the purchasing power of the bond yield. Inflationary expectations are of course built into the original negotiated price and coupon for the bond, but those inflationary expectations may change over time, making the fixed income of the bond look either more or less attractive. This will affect the secondary trading price of the bond on financial markets. An increase in inflationary expectations will cause the trading price of old bonds to fall (as the coupon rate is fixed), and cause the coupon rate on new bonds to rise; both result in higher real yields to the saver that is purchasing a new bond. If you already own a bond and inflation rises more than was expected, then you are in trouble because you are earning less in real terms and the market price of your financial asset is lower. Inflation is thus a second source of risk to bondholders.

7.1.4 Investing in the Stock Market

Rather than owe money to a bank or individual, a firm may choose to sell off part of the firm ownership. One way to do this is by selling *shares* (parts of itself) in the stock market.

There are two types of expected return from owning a share of stock: The first is the expected quarterly dividend payment, the second is the expected future resale price of the stock. Dividend payments are a share of corporate earnings; some firms offer very low or intermittent dividends, while others encourage stock ownership with periodic dividend payments to stockholders. Dividend payments are rarely the primary source of income from owning a stock, however. The primary determinant of the yield from stock ownership is the gap between the expected future sale price and the price the stockholder paid: Ideally, stockholders "buy low" and "sell high" to get the best rate of return.

Stocks, unlike bonds, are not a source of fixed income! Stock market dividends and prices vary considerably over time, and so they are a much riskier type of investment. On the other hand, the value of stocks held generally rise with inflation and so they are a better hedge against inflation risk than are bonds.

The value of trade on the stock market every day depends on the quantity of stocks traded that day as well as on the individual price of each stock traded. Stock prices move because of changes in expectations about the future productivity of the firm (and thus in response to expectations about aggregate MFP) as well as in response to information about expected corporate earnings. A high price-to-earnings ratio means that the stock price is high given current earnings, and it suggests that either the stock is over-valued (people have been paying too much for it) or that people expect *future* earnings (dividends and/or prices) to be higher than they are now.

7.1.4.1 Bubbles and Crashes

The previous paragraph referred to the possibility that stock prices might be over-valued, but it is not obvious how that might happen. Stock market analysts are very rational, and very well-informed about the industries and firms whose stocks they are trading, so how could over-valuation occur? One explanation is that analysts all expect future productivity to be very high, and so they are willing to pay a high price for a stock whose current earnings are low because they are betting the earnings will rise in the future. In that case the price/earnings ratio is high, but the stock is not over-valued.

If however they are wrong, then earnings will not rise and it will turn out that they paid too much for the stock. There are plenty of reasons to think that many analysts could be making the same mistake at the same time and so lead to a sustainable over-valuation of stock prices: The "new economy" period of the 1990s is a nice example, in which people likely over-estimated the impact of high-technology innovations on firm productivity and profits.

On the other hand, there were plenty of nay-sayers during the 1990s that said that the "new economy" was over-rated, and pointed to the flat (or negative) corporate profits of many of the dot-com companies as evidence of a market that was over-saturated with high-tech firms. To those, the incredible growth in stock prices in the 1990s was nothing but a *bubble*—an increase in stock values supported by nothing but the rhetoric (the "hot air") of those that were driving up prices.

In the bubble scenario, people may be buying stocks only to sell them at a higher future price—they are not planning on collecting dividends or even on holding the stock for long enough to find out what future productivity will be. So long as you expect the price to rise, then no matter how much you pay now, you expect to make a profit later. A stock market bubble can exist even if everyone *agrees* the stocks are overvalued, just so long as buyers believe the bubble will last!

Stock market prices can suddenly fall (a stock market *crash*) for reasons similar to the over-valuation story: either because expectations of future productivity fall (rightly or wrongly) or as the result of a "correction" of a stock market bubble, in which stock prices suddenly fall down toward a level more in keeping with actual corporate earnings.

7.2 ARBITRAGE IN FINANCIAL MARKETS

Arbitrage is the process of profit-making. The expression "no arbitrage opportunities" means that there are no profit-making opportunities in the market; in the case of financial markets it means that one cannot make a profit by borrowing cheaply at one place and lending at a high rate someplace else—all rates of return to lending and all costs of borrowing are the same no matter how you do the financing. That of course only happens in equilibrium, but we can predict for example how a stock market bubble should affect bond markets and interest rates by considering how arbitrage will bring us *to* that equilibrium.

Suppose that market analysts begin to be "bullish" about the stock market—their expectations of future dividends begin to rise and so they think the return to holding a stock is rising.[1] People will move their savings into stocks that now offer a higher expected rate of return, and move their savings out of things like bonds and bank accounts, whose expected rates of returns are (as yet) unchanged. At that point, the market is not in equilibrium—an arbitrageur could borrow in the bond market or from a bank at a low cost (low rate of return for a saver) and lend in the stock market (buy stocks) that are offering a higher expected rate of return.

In fact, profit-makers will do exactly that: they will borrow from banks at a low interest rate and use the money to buy stocks. Doing so will make bank loans scarce (demand up, price up) and interest rates will rise toward the expected stock market return—arbitrage profit-making) makes the expected bank and stock returns equalize.

Bond market returns will also begin to rise. Sellers of bonds will be willing to sell at a lower price so that they can get money to put into the stock market. Eventually the sale price falls enough that there is no gain from doing this—arbitrage makes bank, bond, and stock returns equalize.

Even in the absence of arbitrage, rates of return in bond and deposit markets would have risen—higher productivity would affect rates firms were willing to offer in bond and loan contracts. However, arbitrage says something more than that all rates will move together. Arbitrage tells us that all expected rates of return will be *exactly equal* in all markets.

7.3 INTERNATIONAL CAPITAL MARKETS

7.3.1 International Determination of the Real Interest Rate

One aspect of financial assets is that they are traded internationally. If you were to look at a stock or bond market listing, a great many of the financial assets would be foreign. A typical "stock portfolio" will have a mix of developed-economy and "emerging market" stocks. "Emerging markets" are economies whose markets are newly open to international financial inflows, and so economic theory tells us that they may experience very rapid periods of growth as they invest in more and more capital stock.

Asset portfolios are spread across many firms and across many countries. The diversity helps reduce the risk of having all your financial "eggs" in one basket: emerging economies

---

[1]The opposite of a bull market is a bear market—one in which expectations are low.

may follow a bumpy road to growth; economic malaise in the U.S. may not be felt in China; political upheaval in one part of the world may not have the same impact in another part; or Asian exports may grow at the expense of U.S. exports, for example, and so it may be wise to invest in both.

One implication of the free international movement of "capital" (money used to finance investments into the capital stock) is that the arbitrage process outlined in **Section 7.2** will cause expected rates of return to be the same everywhere in the world that allows capital inflows. If expected rates of return are higher in one country than elsewhere in the world, then everyone will want to lend to firms in that country; as Investment increases, diminishing returns will cause rates of return on loans to fall down to world equilibrium levels as the world market returns to equilibrium.

→   Adjusting for risk, expected real rates of return are the same in all countries.

A second implication of the free movement of capital across borders is that domestic savings may be greater than or less than total domestic investment demand; in other words, we may lend more to foreigners than they lend to us, or the reverse could be true.

→   A country may be a net borrower or a net lender in international capital markets.

Figure 1a shows the equilibrium determination of the (risk-adjusted) world real interest rate as the intersection of the Investment Demand and Savings Supply curves just as we derived them in **Chapter 5**; that rate is the same regardless of the method of financing the firm uses to buy the new investment good (uses own savings, borrows from a bank, sells a bond, or sells a stock that pays a dividend). **Figure 1b** shows the level of U.S. Investment demand that exists at that world interest rate. Note that the level of U.S. Investment does not (directly) depend on the level of U.S. savings! All we need to know to determine I(U.S.) is the shape of the U.S. Investment Demand curve and the equilibrium level of the real interest rate.

FIGURE 1a & b:

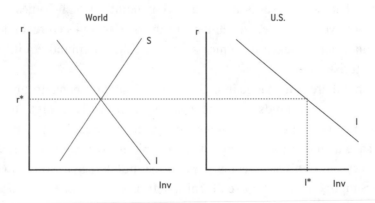

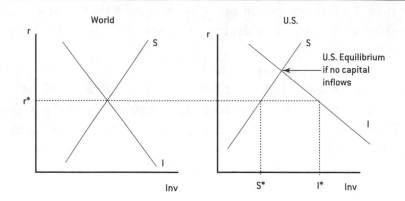

Figures 2a and 2b show the same graph, but also include the U.S. savings supply curve. At the expected rate of return found in **Figure 2a**, U.S. households are not inclined to save as much as U.S. firms want to borrow. U.S. domestic Savings is less than U.S. domestic Investment. In this example, although some of the bonds and stocks sold by U.S. government and by domestic firms are sold to foreign savers, foreigners buy more of our stocks and bonds than we buy of theirs and so we are a *net* borrower. Of course, we are glad of this! If it weren't for those capital inflows, our domestic Investment would be a lot lower—at the level where U.S. Savings Supply intersects U.S. Investment Demand in **Figure 2b**—and so our capital stock and GDP would be a lot lower, too.

The stylized facts of the business cycle described in **Chapter 6** suggested that although shifts in Investment demand are pro-cyclical, movements in the cost of capital are not. This is partly the result of the international nature of capital markets: A shift in Investment demand in the U.S. has only a small impact on world asset prices, and that impact may in some cases be overwhelmed by offsetting factors in other regions of the world.

7.3.1.1 An Example of International Capital Market Arbitrage

Figure 3 illustrates how arbitrage can bring us to an equilibrium like the one shown in **Figure 2**. Imagine that the U.S. starts at an equilibrium point at which domestic Savings Supply is equal to domestic Investment Demand at the worldwide risk-adjusted real interest rate. This would be coincidental, but it makes for a nice starting point. The initial equilibrium values are denoted with an asterisk.

Suddenly there is a change in U.S. household savings behavior; holding rates of return constant, domestic households save less than they used to. This might happen if households were suddenly much more confident about old age Social Security payments (meaning they didn't need to save as much for retirement), or it could happen for demographic reasons—the young and the very old don't save as much as do the middle-aged. But for whatever reason, the U.S. Savings Supply curve in **Figure 3b** shifts left. Loans become more scarce in the U.S., driving up U.S. interest rates. Foreigners want to earn these high rates of return, and so lending to the U.S. increases to take advantage of the relatively high U.S. rate of return.

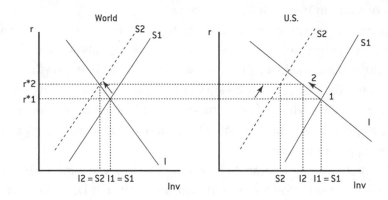

Assume that the change in U.S. Savings behavior is large enough to have some impact on world loan scarcity. When savings leaves other countries to come to the U.S., Savings Supply becomes more scarce in those countries too and it drives up their interest rates as well. The extent to which the U.S. affects world loan scarcity is reflected in the relative magnitude of the shift in World Savings Supply in **Figure 3a.** The shift in *World* Savings Supply looks small relative to the shift in U.S. Savings because the U.S. makes up only a share of World Savings; the smaller we are, the smaller the impact on the World Savings Supply (or World Investment Demand) curve.

In equilibrium, the new world real interest rate is higher, and both World Savings and World Investment are lower as a result of the change in U.S. Savings Supply. U.S. Savings and Investment are also lower than at the initial equilibrium, but the U.S. is now a net borrower in international financial markets.

7.4 THE POVERTY TRAP

Not all countries have free access to international credit markets. For some, lack of access is the result of domestic cultural or political decisions to prevent "foreign control" of the domestic capital stock or to encourage development of a domestic financial base.

Other countries are willing to borrow internationally, but are unable to do so. For some, that is the result of foreign policy (the U.S. has an embargo against loans to Cuba, for example). Other countries with free access to credit markets may appear too risky to foreign investors at *any* nominal interest rate, and so they are in *de facto* capital market isolation.

Capital controls may also interfere with the arbitrage process described in **Section 7.3**. If the domestic government is concerned that is own citizens also think their country is very risky, the country may itself temporarily impose capital controls to prevent all the savings from leaving the economy. If the perception of the country's risk is just a "bubble," then temporarily imposing capital controls until the panic has eased may seem a good idea; on the other hand, capital controls themselves may *fuel* the bubble by making the country seem even riskier to a foreign investor who wants to take their money out and now cannot because of the capital control policy.

Issues about when and if countries should impose capital controls are an important and a popular area of study in international economics.

In general, however, economists agree that the best thing for the economy is to let the market work. For poor countries, access to foreign savings allows them to fund more investments, which allows the capital stock to grow, which leads to GDP growth and income growth. If capital controls exist, then a poor country stays poor because the level of domestic investment is constrained by the savings of poor households; this situation is known as a *poverty trap* because low Savings causes low Investment, which causes income and savings to stay low—the country remains trapped in poverty.

To illustrate the poverty trap, **Figure 4** shows a poor economy with access to gains in MFP and with an educated labor force—in short, with an Investment Demand curve exactly like that for the U.S. in **Figure 2.** Because the economy is poor, however, domestic Savings Supply lies far to the left—at even very high rates of return, total Domestic Savings is relatively low. Because savings is scarce in this economy, the interest rate borrowers have to pay if there are capital controls is much higher than the world interest rate, and so the poverty trap level of investment is quite low.

If capital markets were to be opened, then foreign savings would flow into the economy to take advantage of the high interest offered in the poor economy. As capital flows come in, firms increase their capital stocks and diminishing returns will cause the return on loans to the poor country to fall until the expected real interest paid in that country is equal to the world rate. Equalization of expected world rates of return is the result of international capital market arbitrage. As we move down the developing country Investment Demand curve in this emerging market, there is growth in the capital stock and in GDP.

We can also see in **Figure 4** that the falling expected rate of return also causes a movement down and along the domestic Savings Supply curve—at lower rates of return, households will save less. In fact, however, we know that if the rise in Investment leads to GDP growth, the Savings Supply curve will begin to shift right as household income rises. If the domestic Savings Supply curve shifts rightward (not shown), then the total impact on domestic Savings of opening capital markets will be ambiguous.

FIGURE 4a & b:

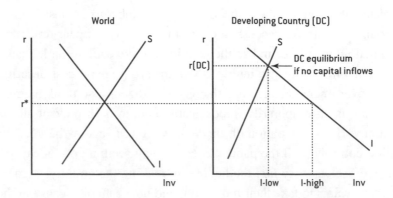

7.5 THEORIES OF U.S. INVESTMENT

One of the stylized facts of the business cycle listed in **Chapter 6** is that Investment spending is pro-cyclical, but much more volatile than GDP. That is not only a feature of the *aggregate* data: Highly disaggregated industry-level data for the U.S. indicate that firm Investment spending tends to be small and fairly smooth for long periods of time, punctuated by large spurts in spending in which more than 10% of the old capital stock is replaced (or added to) at once. In other words, the volatility in the aggregate investment data is also in the firm-level data.

The first stylized fact about Investment spending—that it is pro-cyclical—could easily be attributed to the pro-cyclicality of (measured) MFP. Swings in MFP affect the marginal productivity of capital and therefore cause shifts in the Investment Demand curve. But why is Investment spending so much more volatile than MFP?

One explanation is that when firms want to increase their capital stock, they tend to do it in a big way—they build an entirely new manufacturing plant, for example, rather than add one room to the existing building, or they replace all the typewriters with computer terminals to get full advantage of information processing technologies, rather than replace the typewriters one computer at a time.

→ Making large capital stock adjustments implies physical and organizational costs not included in the cost of capital represented by the real interest rate, and so this type of explanation, while possibly realistic, lies outside our stylized model.

If this is the case in the real world, however, firms will wait and wait until the gains from making a large investment are large enough to cover the costs—they wait and then spend a lot, and they all tend to do it together because all firms tend to face the same market conditions. These factors are graphically represented in our model by shifts in the Investment Demand curve because they affect the level of investment desired at any real interest rate.

A second explanation is that many investments are irreversible, which means that you cannot resell them at the end of the loan period in order to repay your bond or bank debt. Meat lockers, chairs, stamp press machines, tractors, and many other items are easily re-sold, and that is good insurance for a company that takes a loan in a risky economic climate; at the very least, they can sell off the capital stock and repay their debt. The assumption that firms can do that is necessary for the interest rate to be the only cost of borrowing for capital investment. If however a firm invests in research and development and the idea leads nowhere, the investment has no physical product to sell. Less drastically, a lot of capital equipment is "refitted" so that it will be most useful in a firm's production process and would therefore have less value if resold on the market; in that case, the capital is partially irreversible.

→ Full or partial irreversibility is a hidden cost of borrowing to buy a capital good, and so firms will only be willing to invest in irreversible goods if they are very certain of the return; this cost of borrowing is not described explicitly in our model.

During economic downturns, risk is higher for all firms, and so they all postpone irreversible investments. During upswings, trend MFP and GDP looks strong to all firms and so they all individually find it profitable to engage in what might otherwise be risky activity. The real interest rate reflects the markets view of risk in part because it reflects these expectations-related shifts in the Investment Demand curve.

PRACTICE PROBLEMS

1. Draw the U.S. and world markets for capital under the assumption that the U.S. is a net borrower in international capital markets. Assuming that the U.S. is large enough to affect world interest rates, show the impact of a fall in U.S. MFP on the U.S. and world markets for capital. [Hint: you may assume no shift in the Savings curve.]

2. Draw the Swedish market for loans under the assumption that Sweden is a net lender in international capital markets. Show the impact of the change in world interest rates that you described in Question 1 under the assumption that there is no change in Swedish MFP. Does Swedish lending to the U.S. increase or decrease?

3. Your graph from Question 1 may make the change in U.S. borrowing after an MFP decrease look ambiguous, but you can use your answer to Question 2 to explain exactly what happens to U.S. borrowing. Explain.

SUGGESTED ANSWERS

1. MFP falls in the U.S., so mpk falls at any level of Investment and the real interest rate firms are willing to pay falls at any I (Id shifts down). The U.S. is large so Id world shifts down as well. We follow interest determination in the world market: at initial Id, mpk is lower and so the real rate of return earned is lower (perfect competition) and falls to r(temp). At r(temp) households wish they were lending less, and so firms must offer a higher interest rate to attract loans. That requires a higher mpk (perfect comp) and so I falls to get mpk to rise (diminishing returns) until reach a new equilibrium with higher interest rates than r(temp) but lower than where started. Same thing happens in U.S. market, and so S and I are lower in both the U.S. and the world markets.

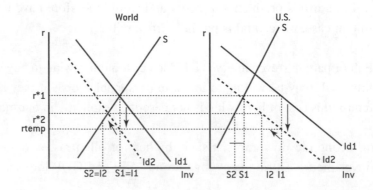

AN INTRODUCTION TO MACROECONOMICS

2. World rates of return fall and so Swedish savers have less incentive to give up consumption and S falls in Sweden. At the same time, Swedish firms are making profits (mpk>r) and so there is entry and I goes up. As I goes up mpk falls (diminishing returns competition) until mpk hits the world interest rate (perfect competition). Swedish lending to the U.S. decreases (savings down but domestic investment demand up in Sweden).

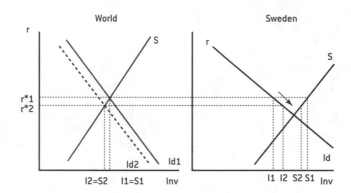

3. U.S. borrowing decreases if Swedish lending to us decreases. This is not surprising—our assets are worth less and so there is less demand by foreigners for them (we don't borrow as much). Remember though that this is all under the assumption that there is no shift in the U.S. Savings curve! U.S. savings might indeed shift to the left if MFP falls because it would be imply lower incomes here and less ability to save at any world interest rate.

THE EXCHANGE RATE

Chapter 7 introduced an international market for financial assets in which money flows across national borders in order to get the highest rate of return. Money that flows into the U.S. from foreign countries affects another market as well however: the market for dollars. U.S. stocks and bonds are valued in dollars, and so foreigners must first buy dollars before they can buy U.S. financial assets. This chapter introduces the market for dollars and how it is affected by foreign demand for our exports and for our assets as well as by our demand for their goods and for their financial assets.

8.1 BALANCE OF PAYMENTS

GDP is measured in two ways: as the sum of all expenditures in the economy (Aggregate Expenditures Approach) and as the sum of all income earned in the economy (Incomes Approach). All payments for goods and services are in turn income to whoever receives the payments, and so the two approaches should in theory yield the same number. Defining Aggregate Income by the letter Y (because I is already taken!) we can therefore write,

$$GDP = Y = C + I + G + X - M$$

Playing with this relationship a little bit, we can track how money enters and leaves the economy through international capital flows and for international trade in goods and services:

$$Y - C - G - I = (X - M)$$

Defining T as the sum of all state, local, and federal taxes, we can insert T into the equation without affecting the sum in the following way:

$$(Y - C - T) + (T - G) - I = (X - M)$$

The first term in the equation is equal to *Household Savings*: it is what is left of income after tax payments and current consumption. It may be positive or negative, depending on whether people are consuming out of current income, borrowing out of future income, or spending out of their accumulated wealth (past savings).

Household Savings = Y – C – T

The second term in the equation is equal to *Public Sector Savings*, also known as *Government Savings*: it is the difference between government tax revenue (government income) and government expenditures. If public sector savings is less than zero, it means that the government is running a *deficit* (spending more than it takes in) and that the deficit is being financed by selling government bonds (by borrowing).

Public Sector Savings = T – G

Aggregate Domestic Savings is just the sum of Household and Public Savings; this "S" corresponds to the domestic "Savings Supply" from **Chapter 7**.

S = Domestic Savings = Household Savings + Public Sector Savings

In **Chapter 7** we focused on the role of the *household* in determining the slope of the Savings supply curve because we believe that Household Savings is the part of S that is sensitive to interest rate changes, whereas public spending decisions are the result of exogenous spending decisions made by governments.

So, we can rewrite our national income accounting identity relating Aggregate Expenditures and Aggregate Income as

(S – I) = (X – M)

The term on the left-hand side of the equation is equal to our net capital flow position and is known as *balance* on the capital account. The term on the right-hand side is our net trade position and is known as the trade balance. Flows of money for the two types of international transactions must be equal—it is just a matter of accounting, not of economics. Because of this, we say there is a *balance of payments* across the country's borders.

8.2 CAPITAL AND TRADE BALANCE SURPLUSES AND DEFICITS

Note that equality between both sides of the Balance of Payments equation implies that

if S < I, then X < M

In words, that means that if members of the European Union are putting money into the U.S. economy in the form of loans to the U.S., then that same amount of money must be leaving our economy on the goods side of the market. Mechanically, Europeans exchange some of their euros for dollars in order to buy our stocks and bonds, and we use the euros we get from them in the exchange to buy their goods. In this example, the dollars flowing in and out of the U.S. economy are balanced, as are the euros flowing in and out of the European Union economy.

Symmetrically,

if S > I, then X > M

If money is leaving the U.S. economy to buy European Union assets, that transaction is balanced by money flowing back in to the U.S. on the goods side of the market. We exchange some of our dollars to get euros so that we can invest in European Union firms and government bonds, and they use the dollars they get from us to buy our export goods.

Balance of payments shows us that the supply of dollars (to get euros) is equal to the demand for dollars (by Europeans) in the dollar-euro exchange market. It is a market of supply and demand for currency (dollars in this case) that brings us to balance of payments equilibrium.

8.2.1 The Capital Account, Current Account, and Trade Balance

International data are grouped into three different categories in the press and in academic literature; they are the capital account, the current account and the trade balance.

We define the *capital account* as the difference between Domestic Savings and Domestic Investment:

S – I = the capital account

We say the capital account is in *surplus* if the amount of money flowing into the economy is *greater* than the amount leaving (S < I), and that the capital account is in *deficit* if the amount of money entering the economy is less than the amount leaving (S > I).

We define the *trade balance* as the difference between exports and imports:

X – M = the trade balance

We say the trade balance is in *surplus* if the money inflows for goods are positive, and that the trade balance is in *deficit* if money outflows are greater than money inflows for goods.

There are two types of international transactions that don't fit neatly into either the trade balance or the capital account. The first are interest and dividend payments on existing loans. They are not financing new capital, and so we want to keep them out of the data that correspond to the Market for Loans in **Chapter 7**. At the same time, they are not payments for goods and services, so they don't belong in the trade balance.

The second type of flow that doesn't fit neatly into either the capital account or trade balance category is called *direct foreign investment*. A loan from an individual is called "direct foreign investment" when the size of the loan to a particular firm is large enough to constitute partial ownership or control of that firm; in that case, the expectation is that the loan money and its dividends will likely remain in the destination country. Examples of direct foreign investments include Korean automakers setting up North American manufacturing plants to get around taxes on car imports—instead of importing the car, we are now importing the car manufacturer.

Because loan payments and direct foreign investments don't fit neatly into either category of the capital account or the trade balance, they are treated separately. In neither case are they flows of money subject to rules of international capital market arbitrage and so they are often lumped with the trade balance in a larger category called the *current account*.

Current account = trade balance + loan payments + direct foreign investment

Following the same conventions as in **Section 8.2.1**, the current account is in *surplus* if more money is entering than leaving the domestic economy, and in *deficit* if more money is leaving than is entering the economy on the current account.

Throughout the text we will ignore the distinction between the current account and the trade balance because our model will not track or explain international interest payments or direct foreign investment spending.

8.3 THE MARKET FOR CURRENCIES

The market for currencies is known as the foreign exchange market. The market for currencies is called an *exchange* market because that is exactly what happens—the only way to buy currency is to offer another currency in exchange.

Currency trades are always between two currencies, therefore exchange rates are *bilateral* things and there are as many U.S. exchange rates as there are other currencies in the world. Because the relative attractiveness of goods and assets varies across countries over time, U.S. exchange rates with different countries won't necessarily all move together—see **Figure 1**.

Very often the press will refer to *the* U.S. exchange rate—when they do that they are usually referring to a trade-weighted price index of all the U.S.'s bilateral exchange rates; the weights used to add up all the bilateral exchange-rates are the share of our total trade that takes place with that particular country (or group of countries, in the case of a monetary union in which

FIGURE 1a: CANADIAN DOLLARS PER U.S. DOLLAR

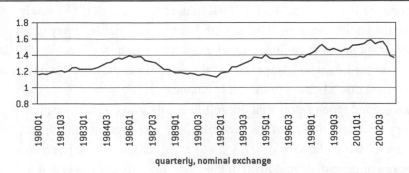

quarterly, nominal exchange

many countries use one currency). A trade-weighted price of the U.S. dollar is also shown in **Figure 1d**.

In this text, the graphical analysis will always consider only bilateral exchange rates.

8.3.1 Why Do People Want to Trade in Currencies?

In our model, there will be three reasons that a foreigner might want to have a U.S. dollar: to import U.S.-made goods from the U.S., to put their savings in U.S. assets, or because they think the exchange value of the dollar may rise in the future (speculation).

FIGURE 1b: BRITISH POUNDS PER U.S. DOLLAR

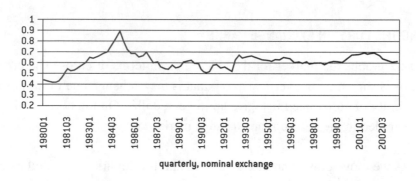

quarterly, nominal exchange

FIGURE 1c: JAPANESE YEN PER U.S. DOLLAR

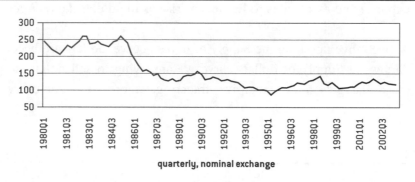

quarterly, nominal exchange

FIGURE 1d: BROAD TRADE-WEIGHTED INDEX OF U.S. DOLLAR

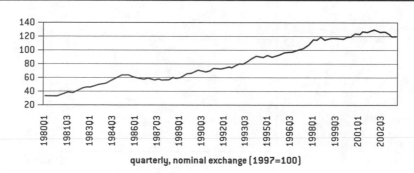

quarterly, nominal exchange (1997=100)

Putting aside speculative reasons, there are two main determinants of the demand for dollars: demand for our exports and demand for our assets.

Foreigners will increase their demand for the dollar if our exports seem relatively cheap or relatively "better" qualitatively. Either case will correspond to a shift in the demand for dollars curve that we'll graph in the next section.

At the same time, a fall in the exchange price of dollars (fewer British Pounds given up in exchange for dollars, for example), will cause our exports to seem cheaper to foreigners (Brits, in this case), and so our exports will rise as a result of a fall in the exchange rate. A change in demand that results from the price change will correspond to a movement along the demand for dollars curve that we'll derive in **Section 8.4**.

Similar relationships apply to asset markets: If foreigners want to buy more U.S. assets, demand for dollars will increase (shift out).

8.4 GRAPHING THE FOREIGN EXCHANGE MARKET

Figure 2 graphs the market for the U.S. dollar in terms of euros. The price of dollars in terms of euros is shown on the vertical axis—that is the exchange rate of dollars in terms of euros, or the quantity of euros one must give up to get a dollar. On the horizontal axis is the quantity of dollars traded in the euro-dollar exchange market.

- As we move down and along the Demand for dollars curve, dollars are becoming cheaper in terms of the number of euros that must be given up in exchange, and so dollar-denominated goods and assets seem cheaper to Europeans; European imports (U.S. exports) and asset sales to Europeans rise as the dollar *depreciates* (falls in value).

- As we move up along the Supply of dollars curve, dollars are becoming more expensive. Along the Supply of dollars curve we are trying to sell dollars to get euros, and so as the dollar gets more expensive, traders get more euros for every dollar traded. Euro-

FIGURE 2:

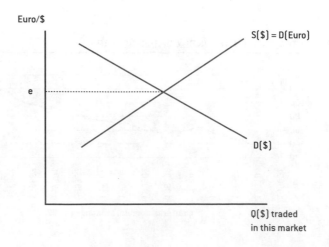

denominated goods and assets seem cheaper to Americans and so U.S. imports rise as the dollar *appreciates* (rises in value).

  ○ The Supply of dollars in this market can be thought of as *our* Demand for euros, as we are only supplying dollars in order to get euros.

Equilibrium is found where the price Europeans (or any traders holding euros) are willing to pay to get our dollars is equal to the price at which we are willing to trade dollars to get euros.

Note that there is no cost function or anything similar behind the concept of a supply curve in the foreign exchange market; we need only understand why currencies are *demanded* in order to understand how the exchange market works.

8.5 MOVEMENTS IN CURRENCY PRICES

Currency demand reflects demand for imports, assets, or speculation that the currency can be sold at a higher price at some point in the future. In equilibrium, expected returns on asset prices are equalized across countries, and so the affects of asset prices on the exchange rate are purely temporary. Similarly, there are no expected future price movements if the currency market is in equilibrium, and so the effects of currency speculation on the exchange are also purely temporary.

8.5.1 Demand for Goods

Demand for goods may change endogenously as currency prices change; this is reflected in a movement along the demand curve.

Things affecting demand for goods that will cause the currency demand curve to *shift* include:

- Change in domestic GDP (which affects income and consumption, some of which is imported)

- Relative price changes between the two countries (making imports seem relative cheap or expensive)

- Taste changes

8.5.1.1 Example: The "Dutch Disease" Scenario of the 1970s
The discovery of natural gas deposits in Holland during the oil crises years of the 1970s led to an incredible surge in demand for the Dutch Guilder in order to buy the relatively cheap fuel source. **Figure 3** plots the theoretical Demand and Supply curves for the Guilder in the dollar-Guilder exchange market. The outward shift in Demand for Guilder causes them to be scarce at the original exchange rate (Demand>Supply) and so the currency appreciates, causing Dutch Exports to fall and Dutch Imports to rise endogenously (as a result of the exchange rate change) to a new equilibrium.

This is known as a "Dutch Disease" scenario because the exchange rate appreciation was very harmful to Dutch exporters that were not in the natural gas industry; there had been no initial increase in demand for their goods, and so the currency price increase caused the rest of the

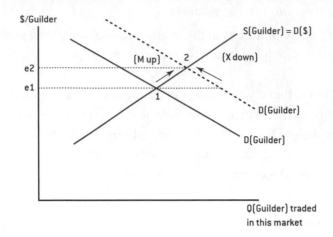

export industry to contract. The expression "Dutch Disease" is often used to describe similar situations in which the success of one export industry has a large impact on the currency price and therefore competitiveness of other industries in the export sector. It is important to note, however, that the economy as a whole is not made worse off—households are able to get imports at relatively low prices, and resources in the long run will move out of uncompetitive export sectors and into natural gas production, where there are high returns to be made.

8.5.2 Demand for Assets

Demand for assets may change endogenously as currency prices change, reflected in movements along the demand and supply for currency.

Things affecting asset demand that will cause the currency demand curve to *shift* include:

- Relative changes in MFP (Investment Demand shifts by more in one country than in the rest)

- Relative changes in expectations about *future* MFP (affecting future dividends and stock and bond prices)

- Relative changes in Savings behavior (household or government)

- Relative changes in expected *future* Savings behavior (affecting future dividends and stock and bond prices)

- Relative changes in perceived Investment risk (affecting arbitrage to equate risk-adjusted expected returns)

- Expected *future* currency price changes (expected rate at which future debt payments will be converted into the domestic currency)

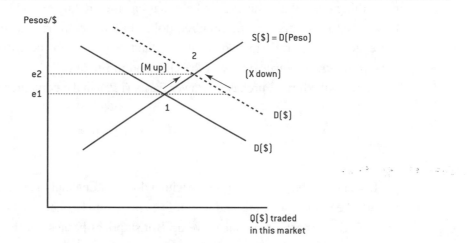

Note that while current currency price changes cause a movement along the curve, future exchange-rate changes are not on the axis and so if they affect demand they cause a shift in the curve.

8.5.2.1 Example: The Dollar Appreciation of the 1990s

U.S. stock prices soared in the latter half of the 1990s on expectation of strong future returns in high technology industries (computers, communications equipment, and semiconductors), despite the fact the current dividend payments and corporate profits in many of the targeted firms were not strong relative to returns on other types of assets in other countries. **Figure 4** plots a theoretical Demand and Supply curve for the U.S. dollar in the peso-dollar exchange market. Demand for dollars shifts out as savers are willing to pay more pesos for every dollar, expecting to make up for the high dollar price with a high future asset return. dollars become relatively scarce (Demand>Supply) and the dollar appreciates, causing U.S. exports to fall and U.S. imports to rise (as pesos now seem relatively cheap).

8.6 LONG-RUN EQUILIBRIUM: PURCHASING POWER PARITY

8.6.1 The Purchasing Power Parity Theory

Although movements in an exchange rate are affected by goods markets, asset markets, and speculation, only goods markets affect the value of a currency in the "long run," when all markets are in equilibrium:

- If asset markets are in equilibrium, there are no changes in capital flows across countries and therefore no changes in currency demand.

- If goods and asset markets are in equilibrium, there is no role for speculation.

In goods market equilibrium, *goods market arbitrage* guarantees that no profits can be made from buying goods in one country and selling them in another. That implies that once we account for the price of currencies, and if we ignore things like tax laws and transportation costs, everything costs the same everywhere that has free and open trade. Another way of putting it is to say that if you took a one-hundred dollar bill and converted it into Pounds, you would have the exact same purchasing power in England as you do in the United States: the dollar would have *purchasing power parity* in the U.S. and in England.

In symbolic form, Purchasing Power Parity (PPP) in the computer industry can be expressed by

$$P_\$^{computers} = \frac{\$}{£} * P_£^{computers}$$

If you could buy more computers with a dollar in England than in the U.S., then big retail stores would take advantage of this and import like crazy from England so that they could sell at high prices in the U.S. This activity would drive up British prices because of the increase in demand for their computers, drive up the cost of the British currency because of the increase in demand for it, and drive down U.S. computer prices because of the decrease in demand for U.S. computers. The act of profit-making would cause the profit opportunity to disappear. We define long-run equilibrium as the point at which such profit opportunities do not exist, and so it is the point at which PPP holds.

The same formula applies to all traded goods in the U.S. and Europe, and so PPP in traded goods can be expressed by

$$P_\$ = \frac{\$}{£} * P_£$$

where the capital letter *P* stands for a traded-goods price index in each country.

Note that goods market arbitrage arguments only apply to certain types of goods:

- PPP only applies to *traded goods*

- The imported and domestically-produced goods must be *identical*

- There can be no taxes or tariffs or transportation costs that cause prices to differ across countries in equilibrium

8.6.2 Relative Purchasing Power Parity

Absolute Purchasing Power Parity may not hold if there are either transportation costs involved from importing goods, or if sales taxes differ across countries. Things like transportation costs and tax differences put a wedge between the domestic and (exchange-rate adjusted) foreign price, but that wedge won't change over time so long as the costs don't change over time. This more realistic form of international goods arbitrage is known as *relative* Purchasing Power Parity.

In symbolic form, Relative Purchasing Power Parity can be expressed by

$$P_\$ = \frac{\$}{£} * P_£ + \text{constant tax differences} + \text{constant transportation consts}$$

Because taxes and transportation costs are different for different pairs of countries and different types of goods, measuring those constant terms can be arduous. Instead, economists tend to look for the existence of Relative PPP by confirming that *changes* in the prices of goods in terms of dollars is exactly equal to *changes* in the import prices once exchange-rate movements are taken into account.

In other words, a simple way to test for Relative Purchasing Power Parity in the data is to see if the following is true:

$$\dot{P}_\$ = \dot{e} + \dot{P}_£ \text{ where } e = \frac{\$}{£}$$

where the "dot" over a variable as usual indicates that it is expressed in growth rates. If transportation costs and tax differences are unchanged (their growth rates are zero), then relative PPP may exist even if absolute PPP does not.

8.6.3 The Real Exchange Rate

It is important to note that the PPP equation doesn't tell us how the economy *gets* to long-run equilibrium; goods market arbitrage could take place only through exchange rate changes, or through only price changes in either or in both countries.

→   PPP is not a theory of long-run exchange-rate determination nor is it a theory of long-run price determination; it can only tell us that in real terms, the equilibrium purchasing power of a dollar should be the same in the U.S. as abroad.

8.6.4 Absolute PPP and Our Macroeconomic Model

We will not consider the impact of taxes on goods and services or transportation costs in our macroeconomic model, and so we will assume that the equilibrium relationship that determines the purchasing power of any currency is described by *absolute* Purchasing Power Parity.

PRACTICE PROBLEMS

The U.S. trade deficit rose in January of 2005 to its second-highest level ever. One contributor was that trade agreements with China allowed for more Chinese imports to be brought into the U.S.

1. Graph the effect of an increase in U.S. demand for Chinese exports on the value of the Yuan in terms of dollars. Explain what exchange-rate policy action the Chinese government would have to use in this case in order to maintain its pegged exchange rate vis-à-vis the dollar and use your graph to show how this policy would work.

2. Use the Purchasing Power Parity equation between China and the U.S. to illustrate the likely impact of Chinese exchange rate policy on inflation rates in China.

SUGGESTED ANSWERS

1. Yuan Demand increases so that the U.S. can get Chinese exports. This will cause an appreciation of the Yuan. To prevent this from happening, China needs a corresponding increase in the supply of Yuan. That will shift out the supply of Yuan curve and cause the exchange rate to fall back to its original level. To do this, the Chinese government uses Yuan to buy dollars (supply of Yuan increases in this exchange market).

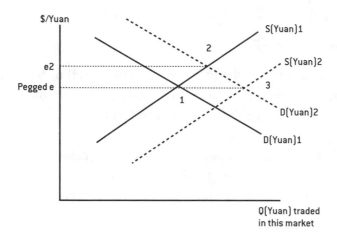

2. P(China)*$/Yuan = P(U.S.). If $/Yuan low then P(China) likely high (assumes Price level in U.S. unaffected by Chinese policy, but it could be a mix of price movements in the two countries.)

AGGREGATE HOUSEHOLD BEHAVIOR

Macroeconomics is the study of the links between microeconomic markets; decision-making by the household links the markets we have studied so far in this text because it is the household labor decision that derives our labor supply curve, the household saving decision that derives our Investment Supply curve, and the household spending decision that affects demand for Imports in our exchange market. Before we can proceed to link these markets, we will spend some time in this chapter discussing the challenges of representing household spending decisions.

The question of how best to represent household behavior is an ongoing area of controversy within the profession. The theory of household behavior that we'll use in our Macroeconomic model will be a hybrid of several different approaches. In some sense that is a real weakness of the theory behind the standard introductory macro model—it is as though we are saying we don't really know what is going on! On the other hand, this model will be flexible enough that we can use it to illustrate the views of several "camps" of macroeconomists and policymakers; you'll be able to form your own opinion about what you think is the "right" way to describe household behavior.

9.1 ARE HOUSEHOLDS ECONOMICALLY "RATIONAL"?

Imagine that "household x" wins an after-tax lottery prize of $1 million. It might be tempting to run out and spend it all at once on trips to Paris and expensive clothes, and in fact some households no doubt would do just that! A *rational* household would consider this a one-million-dollar increase in its lifetime earnings; it would spend some now, and save (and earn interest on) the rest. That would allow the household to consume more every year for the rest of its (expected) lifetime. Being rational doesn't sound like as much fun, but that would clearly be the smart thing to do—the household would reconsider how much it had to save for all of its future child care, hospital, housing, and retirement expenditures, and then it would adjust its planned consumption in each period accordingly.

To summarize the previous paragraph: In response to a temporary increase in income today, the rational household would increase its consumption in every period into the future by the same amount, whereas an irrational household might increase consumption by a lot today, and then fall back down to the old level for every year in the future.

Now, business cycles are by definition temporary deviations in Aggregate Income. How does Consumption change in response to these temporary changes in income? That depends on whether people are rational! If they are rational, the household knows the business cycle is a temporary thing and it will save during booms and spend out of savings during recessions. If households are irrational, then aggregate C will rise during booms and fall during recessions.

Moreover, if households are irrational, they *exacerbate* business cycles by causing spending to fall in response to a fall in income; by spending less, they cause other people's income to fall even further and so those people spend even less and so on. If households are irrational, then business cycles are bigger than they would be if people were rational and kept their spending "smooth" over the cycle.

9.2 WHY CAN'T ECONOMISTS DECIDE WHETHER OR NOT HOUSEHOLDS ARE RATIONAL CONSUMERS?

9.2.1 The Data

What is "expected" lifetime income? In the 1990s there was a boom in the information-technology sector; many people believed it was a "bubble," whereas many others believed we had entered a "new economy" period of sustainable rapid economic growth; both types of people had rational arguments behind their views, but the implications for rational household behavior were different—the first group would have saved a lot in the 1990s whereas the second group would not have. Even now it is hard to say who was right! But let us assume that it was in fact a bubble. In the data, the people who spent a lot as their incomes rose would look irrational, but in fact they may have been rational agents that just made a mistake that they are unlikely to make again.

A second factor that makes the data hard to interpret is that rational goals may be *constrained* in some way. For example, some households may rationally want to borrow money during a recession and then pay it back during the following (expected) recovery, but they can't get a loan. In other words, credit market constraints may force people to consume out of their current, rather than future, income. Credit market constraints don't apply to everyone in the economy, but they may be enough to affect the Aggregate Consumption data.

The data *do* tell us that Aggregate Consumption is smoother than Aggregate Income, so that is some support for the rationality camp. On the other hand, changes in Aggregate Consumption also seem to respond to temporary changes in Aggregate Income—that could be evidence of either credit constraints or of irrational behavior.

In other words, the Aggregate Consumption and Aggregate Income data can be interpreted as lending support to both theories.

9.2.2 The Theory

Household behavior is more difficult to tie down than firm behavior because there are no competitive forces that guarantee that all households will, in equilibrium, behave in the same way. To illustrate: we know that in equilibrium the expected return from a capital investment must be the same for every firm in the economy: this is the case because if returns were higher at any one firm, savers would only allocate their money to that one firm and either diminishing returns would drive down the productivity of capital of that firm, or the other firms would go out of business. All firms are forced to drive their marginal profits to zero as a result of the twin assumptions of perfect competition and the diminishing returns. We can disagree about how long it takes the economy to get to equilibrium, but economists are unlikely to disagree about how that equilibrium will look. There is nothing comparable for household theory—households that manage their finances poorly are not driven from the economy in equilibrium, and so nothing forces all households to behave in the same way in equilibrium.

If indeed people are irrational in their spending patterns, by which we mean they do not behave like logical, forward-looking, economic agents, is there any way of saying what they will do? In other words, how do we model "irrationality"? People could do anything! That sort of modeling assumption would get us nowhere as economic theorists—behavior would be completely unpredictable.

Rather than throw up our hands in despair, economists generally model irrationality in one of two ways; they either assume that people follow a rule of thumb and consume a constant fraction of their income (and save the rest) every period, or that they think that future conditions will look exactly like the recent conditions. In either case, we assume that irrationality follows a particular rule—this ties down the model and allows us to predict behavior, but these assumptions are neither more nor less justified by the data than is the rationality assumption.

9.3 THREE MODELS OF HOUSEHOLD BEHAVIOR

9.3.1 Rational Households

Rational households forecast all of their future earnings from labor income and from interest on savings, taking into account when they plan to retire. The sum of all of those earnings, net of expected taxes, is "expected lifetime disposable income" (income left for their disposal after tax payments). Expected lifetime flows of disposable income sum to total expected lifetime *wealth*. *Expected* lifetime wealth may not be what actually happens, but the household makes its best forecast.

This calculation of expected lifetime wealth reflects their expected future labor decisions about how much to work and how much leisure time to take in every single period for the rest of their lives. If households do this exactly correctly, and if they forecast both their retirement age and years of life in retirement, then they will consume the same amount and have the same standard of living in every year until they die (or until their expectations of their future lifetime income changes!).

Now, this "rational agent" is beginning to sound like some sort of economic super-hero, but in fact many people do save for retirement, and they do so trying to forecast how many years they will be in retirement (how long they think they'll live) as well as any expected future costs they might have or expenditures they might want to make in those retirement years. When people have children, they adjust their spending forecast and often start socking money away immediately for expected future expenditures on school, orthodonture, and so on.

Now, if households are rational and forward-looking, they know that there will be good times (Y above trend) and bad times (Y below trend) and they will do their best to smooth their Consumption over those good and bad times—saving during good times and consuming out of savings during bad times. In other words, if households are rational then Consumption spending should be very smooth over the business cycle and not be sensitive to temporary changes in income.

9.3.2 Rational Households with Credit Constraints

These types of rational households also forecast their lifetime earnings and labor decisions, and they also try to keep their Consumption spending as smooth as possible, but they've had the bad luck to encounter their first economic downturn before they could accumulate sufficient savings and also before they have been able to establish a good credit rating. They know that the economic downturn is temporary and they know that they should rationally borrow from a bank and pay it back in the future during the eventual economic upturn, but they can't get the loan; they are *credit constrained*. Because they are credit constrained, their Consumption will fall as their income falls in the temporary downturn, and Consumption may not be much smoother than GDP over the business cycle.

Now, it is a bit more complicated to use the credit constraint model to explain why Consumption might *rise* as income temporarily rises—only people working in underground (illegal) businesses are unable to *save* money through traditional channels when income rises. One story is that households that have postponed purchases of durable consumption goods like cars, refrigerators, and so on, will suddenly buy a lot of those things once their incomes start to rise—they are just rationally compensating themselves for the delay in utility forced upon them by the credit constraints they faced during the previous downturn. Thus credit constraints may cause Consumption spending to "spurt" or rise immediately as the economy exits a recession.

9.3.3 Irrational Households that Follow a "Rule of Thumb"

Households may not be as rational and forward-looking as economic reasoning would suggest. They may instead just follow a simple rule of thumb in which they save a constant fraction of every paycheck for retirement and for emergency spending, and they spend the rest. They do not try to forecast future income or future borrowing or retirement needs at all precisely, nor do they try to smooth their consumption. They might save, for example, 10% of every paycheck with a sort of vague sense that "this should be enough." During economic booms, they buy expensive houses and fast cars, and during economic recessions they have to sell off those possessions and buy fewer goods because they don't have sufficient savings to allow for consumption-smoothing.

Now, nobody wants to be called an "irrational agent," but many people do indeed follow a rule of thumb in terms of their expenditures, and even the rich and famous often seem unprepared for what seem to be fairly predictable variations in their lifetime income! "Rule of thumb" households may cause Consumption spending to be highly correlated with temporary movements in GDP.

9.4 A HYBRID DESCRIPTION OF HOUSEHOLD SPENDING

The economy may be made up of a mix of rational, rational-but-credit-constrained, and rule-of-thumb households. Even rule-of-thumb households save income, and so all households can consume even when their incomes are zero (for instance in retirement). We will denote the part of Consumption spending that doesn't depend on temporary swings in disposable income as the exogenous component of Consumption spending. The second term in the Consumption equation represents the sensitivity of current spending to *temporary* fluctuations in disposable income, measured by the "marginal propensity to consume" out of disposable income.

$$C = \bar{C} + mpc * (Y - T)$$

where

- Y represents temporary deviations from trend Aggregate Income.

- mpc stands for the "marginal propensity to consume" out of temporary fluctuations in *disposable* (after tax) income.

- $\bar{C}$ is known as the exogenous component of Aggregate Consumption—one part of C that does not depend on (is exogenous with respect to) temporary movements in GDP (Y).

- T stands for Taxes paid; taxes are assumed for simplicity not to depend on income.

The marginal propensity to consume reflects the joint importance of irrationality and credit constraints. If the marginal propensity to consume is greater than zero, then we can say that Consumption is a *function* of temporary changes in GDP.

A graph of the Consumption Function is just a graph of C with Y (equals GDP) on the horizontal axis (see **Figure 1**). The slope is the marginal propensity to consume (how much C rises for any change in GDP). The intercept is equal to $\bar{C} - mpc*T$—that is, the level of C when disposable GDP is equal to its trend level. It is also the level of C if all households are rational and without credit constraints (i.e. when mpc = 0).

Things that will shift the Consumption function are the things that affect expected lifetime disposable income; in our Aggregate model, that boils down to correct and incorrect expectations about MFP (which affects returns to both labor and investment income) and to correct and incorrect expectations about lifetime taxation.

Note that the slope of the Consumption Function depends on the extent of credit constraints *and/or* irrationality in the economy. If everyone is rational and there are no credit constraints, then mpc = 0, $C = \bar{C}$, and the Consumption function is perfectly flat. The only time there would be a change in C in that case would be if there were a change in expected lifetime income or a permanent expected change in taxation.

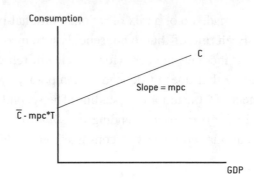

PRACTICE PROBLEMS

Assume that it is widely reported in the news media that the government will need to raise taxes in the next few years.

1. What will be the impact on current consumption and savings if households are perfectly rational and face no credit constraints? Explain.

2. What will be the impact on current consumption and savings if households are perfectly rational but are currently credit constrained? Explain.

3. What will be the impact on current consumption and savings if households are irrational and follow a rule of thumb in their spending decisions? Explain.

SUGGESTED ANSWERS

1. Rational households will expect that their lifetime disposable incomes will be lower following the future tax increase, and so they will reduce their consumption now so that they won't have to make an even larger reduction in utility in the future. Current savings increases to help out with future consumption and tax bills.

2. Credit constrained households already have reduced Consumption because they are credit constrained. The expected future tax increase will therefore have no effect on current consumption and savings behavior unless they have to pare back spending even further than current levels.

3. Households that follow a rule of thumb set current savings and consumption as a constant fraction of current disposable income. They are aware of the likelihood of a future tax increase but don't change their current behavior. That is why they are labeled "irrational"—they have the information but they ignore it. In this case there is no change in current Consumption or Savings.

DERIVING AGGREGATE SUPPLY AND AGGREGATE DEMAND

We finally have all the pieces together that we need for our integrated macro model of the economy! In this chapter we'll use the theories that we've seen so far to derive the Aggregate Demand and Aggregate Supply curves that we'll use in later chapters to represent business cycle movements, long-run changes in economic conditions, and the effects of macroeconomic policy-making on the aggregate economy.

When we look at Aggregate Demand and Aggregate Supply, we will be using them to understand *cyclical* changes in the economy. It is important to remember that we'll be ignoring "trend" or "permanent" changes in GDP and natural income while doing so.

10.1 AGGREGATE DEMAND AND AGGREGATE SUPPLY

Aggregate Demand is defined as any *planned* change in the Aggregate Expenditure components of GDP defined in Chapter 3.

$$\text{Aggregate Demand} = \text{Consumption} + \text{Planned Investment} + \text{Government} + \text{Exports} - \text{Imports}$$

In other words,

$$\text{Aggregate Demand} = \text{Aggregate Expenditures} - \text{unplanned changes in inventory investment}$$

Another way of saying this is that

$$\text{Aggregate Demand} = \text{GDP} - \textit{unplanned changes in inventory investment}$$

where Gross Domestic Product is, by definition, equal to Aggregate Supply in a given time period. If Aggregate Demand is greater than Aggregate Supply (greater than GDP), then firms must be selling out of inventories in a way they hadn't anticipated. If Aggregate Demand is less than Aggregate Supply (less than GDP), then firms must be accumulating inventories faster than they had planned.

This means that Aggregate Supply and Aggregate Demand are equal only when the goods market is in equilibrium—the point in the market where no one wishes they had produced more or less. Equilibrium is the point where there is no unplanned accumulation or reduction in inventory investment.

10.2 THE AGGREGATE DEMAND CURVE

The Aggregate Demand (AD) curve is a graphical representation of the tradeoff between Planned Aggregate Expenditures and the Aggregate Price Index P, which we measure in the data by the CPI. Because Planned AE equals GDP in equilibrium, we will graph this as a relationship between P and the demand for GDP (and put GDP on the horizontal axis). As with any graphical representation, things that affect the curve that are on the axes affect the *slope* of the curve; things that affect the curve that are not on the axes cause the curve to *shift*.

10.2.1 Changes in the Price Level and the Slope of AD

There are three principal reasons that Aggregate Demand increases as the Price level falls:

1. *The international substitution effect*: As the U.S. price level falls, our exports seem cheaper to foreigners and X rises; at the same time, foreign products seem relatively more expensive (than U.S.-made products), and so M falls. Both the increase in X and the decline in M have a positive impact on U.S. Aggregate Demand.

2. *The intertemporal substitution effect*: If prices are temporarily lower in the current time period than they are expected to be in the future, then households and firms will move up their consumption of some durable goods before the future expected price increase.

3. *The real wealth effect*: Holding lifetime expected income constant, lower prices means greater purchasing power, and so spending by households and firms will increase.

All three factors suggest a down-sloping relationship between Aggregate Expenditures and the Price Level, as shown in **Figure 1**. (Note that we may put GDP on the horizontal axis rather than "Aggregate Expenditures" as the two are equal in equilibrium.)

10.2.2 Shifts in the Aggregate Demand Curve and the Aggregate Expenditure Multiplier

AD shifts if there is a change in spending *at any price*. To consider what shifts AD, consider that total planned AE in the economy is the sum of each of the AE components.

AD = Consumption + Planned Investment + Government + Exports + Imports

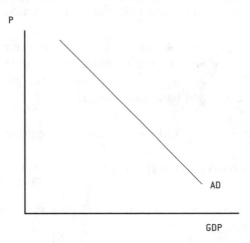

We've seen models that determine spending levels for each component other than Government spending, which we'll save for later chapters. One thing that is clear is that these AE components affect each other: changes in I, G, X, and M affect GDP, which in turn affects C via the Consumption Function:

$$C = \bar{C} + mpc * (Y - T)$$

$$C = \bar{C} + mpc * (AE - T)$$

Assuming that a constant fraction of Consumer goods are imported, this also implies that Imports are a function of GDP. We can write

$$M = \overline{M} + mpm * (Y - T)$$

$$M = \overline{M} + mpm * (AE - T)$$

where

- $\overline{M}$ is the exogenous part of imports that varies with the exogenous component of Consumption, with Investment imports, or with changes in the cost of the Dollar.

- mpm is the *marginal propensity to import* out of temporary changes in disposable income.

and where the marginal propensity to import is less than or equal to the marginal propensity to consume.

Putting this all together, the Aggregate Demand curve is a graphical representation of the following equation:

$$AD = \bar{C} + mpc * (AE - T) + planned\ I + G + X - \overline{M} - mpm * (AE - T)$$

We can solve for the equilibrium level of AD by using the fact that Aggregate Expenditures are just equal to AD plus any unplanned changes in inventories.

$$AD = \overline{C} + mpc * (AD + \text{unplanned chages in inventories} - T) + \text{planned I} + G$$
$$+ X - \overline{M} - mpm * (AD + \text{unplanned changes in inventories} - T)$$

Collecting terms on the right hand side, we have

$$AD = \overline{C} + (mpc - mpm) * (AD + \text{unplanned } \Delta\text{inventories} - T) + \text{planned I} + G + X - \overline{M}$$

And then we can solve for AD in the following two steps:

$$AD * [1 - (mpc - mpm)] = \overline{C} + \text{planned I} + G + (mpc - mpm) * (\text{unplanned } \Delta\text{inventories} - T)$$
$$+ \overline{X} - \overline{M}$$

$$AD = \frac{1}{1 - (mpc - mpm)} * \{\overline{C} + \text{planned I} + G + (mpc-mpm)*(\text{unplanned inventories} - T)$$
$$+ \overline{X} - \overline{M}\}$$

Now the equilibrium level of AD is just a function of the equilibrium levels of C, I, G, X and M we've determined elsewhere in the text, as well as the degree of irrationality and credit constraints in the economy (mpc) net of their influence on foreign economies (mpm).

In equilibrium, any change in the value of $\overline{C}$, T, planned I, G, X, or $\overline{M}$ will have a *multiplied* effect on Aggregate Demand so long as the first term in the equation

$$(\frac{1}{1 - (mpc - mpm)})$$

is greater than 1. That term—known as the "Aggregate Expenditure Multiplier"—will be larger the larger the marginal propensiy to consume. If people are perfectly rational, then mpc=mpm=0 and the multiplier is equal to one. Otherwise, the more irrational or credit-constrained people may be, the larger the mpc and the larger the total change in spending as people react to changes in their income.

Shifts in the AD curve will be larger the larger is the Aggregate Expenditure Multiplier. Shifts in AD will be larger if[1]

- The marginal propensity to consume is large (people are either irrational or credit constrained)
  - An exogenous change in one part of the economy causes Consumption to change in the same direction, so the total change (shift) in AD is equal to the initial change plus the change in Consumption (larger if mpc is larger)

---

[1]Note that shifts in the AD curve will be smaller the more of the exogenous changes in $\overline{C}$, T, planned I, G, X, and $\overline{M}$ are met by endogenous unplanned inventory adjustments. Thus we can only say that the shift in the AD curve (increase in AD at any price level) in response to an exogenous change will be larger the larger the expenditure multiplier; we cannot at this point define the exact size of the shift in the AD curve.

AN INTRODUCTION TO MACROECONOMICS

- The marginal propensity to import is small (where mpm is less than or equal to the mpc)
  - The more of the endogenous change in Consumption is imported, the less of an impact the endogenous response will have on Aggregate Demand for *domestically*-produced goods (the smaller the AD shift)
    - Note: if mpc=mpm, then the multiplier equals 1 even if both mpc and mpm are greater than zero; in this case there is no multiplied effect on domestic Aggregate Demand because the change in Consumption is exactly offset by a change in Imports.

10.3 LONG-RUN DETERMINATION OF GDP

The production function for GDP has three inputs in our model: MFP, L, and K. We assume that MFP is always equal to its long-run equilibrium value (there is no market for MFP).

Moreover, we have already derived the long-run equilibrium levels of the labor and capital inputs in **Chapter 4** of the text; we did not need to know anything about the Price level in order to find equilibrium in the labor or capital markets, and so we know that the long-run equilibrium level of GDP does not depend on the Price level. That is because any change in P is matched by a change in Wages to make w/p = mpl at equilibrium employment, and because any change in inflation is matched by a change in nominal interest rates to make r = mpk at equilibrium levels of Investment.

We know that no matter what happens to Aggregate Demand or labor markets over the business cycle, the economy will eventually return to the long-run level of GDP determined by labor and capital market equilibrium. It is sometimes helpful to see what that long-run equilibrium level of GDP is when we are graphing things, and so it is represented graphically by a vertical line. The line is vertical because Long-Run Aggregate Supply does not depend on the Price Level—in the Long-Run GDP is the same at any price (**Figure 2**).

Long-Run Aggregate Supply (LRAS) is often referred to as *potential* or *trend* GDP: it is the level of GDP implied by trend growth in MFP, K, and L.

In our de-trended model, changes, or shifts, in LRAS reflect changes in MFP, equilibrium L, and the equilibrium K-stock; the corresponding change in the real-world data would be a change in trend GDP growth.

FIGURE 2:

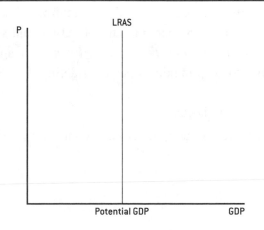

10.4 AGGREGATE SUPPLY

There are three inputs into the production of GDP: MFP, K, and L. We assume that MFP is always in equilibrium, and that capital market arbitrage works immediately to always keep capital markets in equilibrium. That implies that *any cyclical changes in GDP must be the result of cyclical changes in employment*. The Aggregate Supply (AS) curve plots the *short-run* relationship between Prices and GDP, and it is derived from a *short-run* relationship between Prices and employment.

10.4.1 Changes in the Price Level and the Slope of AS

In **Chapter 4** we derived a downward-sloping labor demand curve using the twin assumptions of diminishing returns and perfect competition. We will use our theory about that labor demand curve to derive an upward-sloping short-run relationship between the aggregate Price Level and production.

Perfect competition in the labor market implies

$$\frac{w}{p} = mp1$$

To derive the slope of the AS curve, we want to see how the labor input responds to changes in the Price Level *only*. The point is to see how AS changes as P changes while holding everything else constant—that will give us the slope of the AS curve. Anything else that affects Labor demand will shift the AS curve—we'll soon see an example!

Consider the case where the Price level *increases*. Holding nominal wages (W) constant, that means that the purchasing power of wages is falling (w/p falls). Under perfect competition, that can only happen if the marginal productivity of labor is falling (mpl falls). Under the assumption of diminishing returns, mpl falls as the Labor input increases. If Labor is increasing as P increases, then we know from our production function that GDP is increasing as P increases. That implies that AS is upward-sloping: GDP rises as P rises (holding everything else constant).

Another, less mathematical, way of thinking about the upward-sloping AS curve is as follows: If firms want to increase output, they must increase their labor input: the marginal productivity of labor falls because of diminishing returns. That means that they have to pay for more hours of work for every marginal unit of output, and so their costs and prices must rise *even if they pay workers the same hourly wage* (w is unchanged).

Important things to keep in mind when considering the AS curve are

- Only the labor input is changing
  - K and MFP are constant, therefore any increase in GDP results in diminishing returns to L.

- Nominal wages are held constant
  - Changing costs are solely the result of diminishing returns—only the result of changing output, which is on the axis.

10.4.2 Shifts in the Aggregate Supply Curve

Aggregate Supply shifts any time there is a change in

- MFP or K

- Nominal Wages

The Aggregate Supply curve is derived from the Labor Demand curve; anything that shifts the labor demand curve (change in MFP or change in K) will shift the Aggregate Supply curve; it implies a higher or lower level of employment and therefore of GDP at any price.

Changes in nominal Wages (W) shift AS because they affect the prices firms must charge to cover costs at any level of output. A change in W is a movement along Labor Demand because real wages (W/P) are on the axis in that graph. Wages are not on the axis of the AS graph, and so they are exogenous to the AS-AD graph; exogenous variables are ones that shift the curve.

PRACTICE PROBLEMS

It is by no means obvious that the Social Security system we have now will ever run out of money, or that we will ever need to make cutbacks in Social Security benefits paid to retirees. However, most people seem to think that there will be cutbacks in what we do receive in Social Security benefits upon retirement. For what follows, assume that everyone believes that Social Security retirement benefits will be cut in the future. [You may ignore any secondary impact this forecast has on household forecasts about the government budget deficit or on tax policy.]

FIGURE 3:

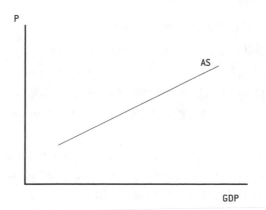

1. Assuming that all households follow a rule of thumb in their consumption decisions...

    a. What will be the impact on current Consumption expenditures? Explain.

    b. Will the impact on Aggregate Demand be larger or smaller than the impact on Consumption? Explain.

2. Assuming that all households are perfectly rational and have no credit constraints...

    a. What will be the impact on current Consumption expenditures? Explain.

    b. Will the impact on Aggregate Demand be larger or smaller than the impact on Consumption? Explain. (No formulas are required.)

    c. What will be the impact on current world real interest rates (assuming the U.S. is large enough to affect world rates)? Explain briefly. (No graph required.)

SUGGESTED ANSWERS

1. Rule of thumb households...

    a. There will be no change in current consumption or savings because there is no change in current disposable income, and these households only base their spending decisions on what they currently observe.

    b. The change in AD is equal to the change in Consumption times the multiplier. The multiplier is greater than 1 in this case, but the change in Consumption is equal to zero! That means that the change in AD equals the change in Consumption—neither moves at all.

2. Perfectly rational and unconstrained ...

    a. C will fall because expected lifetime disposable income is lower, meaning lifetime C flows must be lower.

    b. The impact on AD is exactly equal to the change in Consumption. The mpc is equal to zero (as is mpm) and so the multiplier is equal to "one." The change in AD = change in C.

    c. Savings rises because households are savings for retirement. The increase in savings, assuming we are large enough to affect world interest rates, makes loans less scarce and so world real interest rates fall.

MACROECONOMIC ADJUSTMENT IN THE AS-AD MODEL

Now we're ready to really use the model! Take a deep breath—integrating all of the different micro markets into two graphs sounds like a great simplification, but actually there is a lot to keep track of along the way and it can get pretty complicated. The payoff is worth it though: We can use the model to ask a variety of interesting questions about the economy—including questions about the usefulness (and lack thereof!) of policymaking.

11.1 LONG-RUN GOODS MARKET EQUILIBRIUM

The goods market is in equilibrium when Aggregate Supply equals Aggregate Demand and there are no unplanned changes in inventories. The goods market is in *long-run* equilibrium when Aggregate Supply equals Aggregate Demand at potential GDP; that is a long-run equilibrium because at that point all goods and input markets are in equilibrium at once. At that point, there is no reason for firms to change their production plans or employment plans.

Long-run goods market equilibrium is depicted graphically in **Figure 1**, where an asterisk is used to denote equilibrium points, and GDP* indicates the long-run equilibrium point known as potential GDP.

11.2 ADJUSTMENT IN GOODS AND LABOR MARKETS TO AN AD SHOCK

A *shock* to an economic system is an unexpected exogenous change in a variable. Shocks are things that shift the curves. In the case of Aggregate Demand, potential

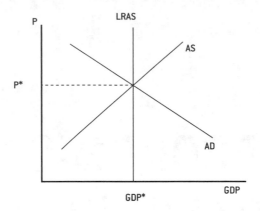

shocks include changes in expectations about future income (whether or not those expectations are accurate), exogenous changes in world interest rates (that do not result from shifts in domestic Investment Demand or Supply), a change in Government spending or Taxation, a change in the price of the dollar in terms of other currencies, an exogenous change in demand for our exports or for imports, or a change in expected or current MFP (that would affect both Consumption and Investment demand).

The dynamics we'll go through below can be a bit overwhelming, but the good news is that these are the tools and graphs we'll use throughout the rest of the course—no new graphs or markets to learn after this.

11.2.1 Example: An Exogenous Increase in Demand for Exports

Starting from an initial Long-Run equilibrium denoted by the number "1," there is a positive shock to exports. This may result from an increase in foreign income, or from a change in world preferences for our goods.

The AD curve shifts to the right; AD is higher at any Price. The AD shift is larger the larger the expenditure multiplier. That shift is shown in **Figure 2**.

At P1, AD>AS and so we know that there is an unplanned decrease in inventories; there is as yet no change in AS, and so there is no immediate change in GDP or labor demand.

Firms realize the magnitude of the AD shock when their inventories start to decumulate. Moreover, scarcity of goods starts to put upward pressure on prices. Under perfect competition, firms will either immediately increase their production in response to the price incentive, or there will be entry.

In either case, more workers need be employed to produce the additional output, and the rise in price, under perfect competition, exactly compensates for rising costs from diminishing returns in the labor market. Rising prices in the goods market reflect increased production and a movement along the AS curve toward point 2 in **Figure 2**.

At the same time, the increase in prices chokes off some of the initial AD shock and results in a movement along the AD curve toward point 2. AD falls back toward point 2 because of the

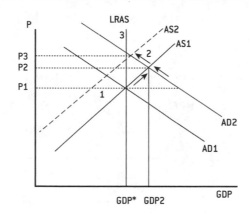

inter-temporal substitution, international substitution, and real wealth effects described in **Chapter 10**.

At point 2, the goods market is in equilibrium—there are no unplanned changes in inventories where AS=AD. Both GDP and Prices have increased.

However, labor markets are *not* in equilibrium at point 2, as shown in **Figure 3**. Rising Prices and Output have resulted in a movement down and along the labor demand curve to a lower marginal productivity of labor, a lower real wage (as the denominator has risen), and a higher level of employment (corresponding to a higher level of GDP in **Figure 2**).[1]

Point 2 is not a labor-market equilibrium because at the current level of employment, workers are not getting compensated enough for the higher level of labor they are providing: the opportunity cost of labor in terms of leisure foregone is greater than the real wage at point 2.

Workers either quit or demand a higher nominal wage to compensate them for the higher price level. If workers quit, the fall in employment will result in a higher marginal productivity of labor and, under perfect competition, firms will offer a higher *nominal* wage in compensation (causing real wages to increase). If workers demand a higher nominal wage, then firms must lay off workers in order to cover the higher cost, and again the mpl rises at the same time as the real wage increase under perfect competition.

In either case, the labor market moves back along the labor demand curve toward point 3 until it reaches an equilibrium back at the initial real wage and initial level of employment.

In goods markets, rising nominal wages causes the AS curve to shift upward and to the left: at any level of output, firms must charge higher prices in order to cover higher wage costs. As the AS curve shifts leftward, increased scarcity causes goods prices to rise and for Aggregate Demand to fall endogenously in response to the price change (as a result of international, inter-temporal, and real wealth effects). As the labor market returns to long-run equilibrium and the original level of employment, the goods market returns to long-run equilibrium and the initial level of output at point 3.

---

[1]Remember that employment and real wages are always determined by the labor demand curve in this model—the labor demand curves shows the level of real wages at any level of employment under the assumption of perfect competition, and perfect competition always holds in this model.

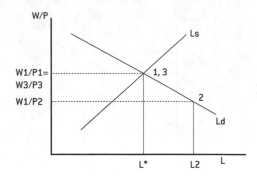

Note that in **Figure 3** we have assumed that wages and prices adjust together in one step from point 2 to point 3 to return the labor market to equilibrium. That assumption is just a simplification of the model dynamics. In fact, nothing in our model tells use how quickly the economy will adjust to a new Long-Run Equilibrium; we can only say what that equilibrium will look once we get there.

11.2.2 The General Case of an AD Shock

Labor and goods market adjustments will look the same regardless of the source of the economic shock. In other words, all positive AD shocks look the same as each other so long as they are not associated with changes in MFP (LRAS). All negative AD shocks will look the same as each other; the dynamics of a negative AD shock will be symmetric to the case in **Section 11.2.1**.

- AD shocks that are unrelated to changes in MFP will have no impact on Output or Employment in the Long Run. Positive AD shocks will only be inflationary in the Long Run; Negative AD shocks will only be deflationary in the Long Run.

The stages of adjustment are the same whether the AD shock is positive or negative:

- AD shifts; there is no initial change in GDP or Prices.

- There are unplanned changes in inventories that signal to firms the direction of Price and Output changes.

- Firms adjust Prices and Employment simultaneously as we move simultaneously along both the labor demand and AS curves.

- The change in Prices causes an endogenous change in AD (movement along AD).

- Goods market equilibrium is achieved where AS=AD at a new level of Output and Prices; Labor markets are in disequilibrium (we are not at full employment and workers are not getting compensated appropriately for the value of their leisure).

- Nominal Wage and Employment adjust to Labor market equilibrium.

- The change in nominal wages shifts the AS curve as costs change at any level of output; the resulting change in Prices causes a second endogenous movement along the AD curve until the goods market returns to equilibrium.

- Prices and nominal Wages have changed one-for-one. There are no changes in *real* variables: real wages return to their original level, as do employment and GDP.

11.3 ADJUSTMENT IN GOODS AND LABOR MARKETS TO AN AS SHOCK

We will restrict our study of AS shocks to changes in expected or actual MFP, as that is the ultimate source of employment and capital stock growth in our model.

Any time there is a change in MFP (expected or actual), there are both AD and AS influences. Everything shifts! However, in terms of model tractability there are a few bits of good news:

- We will always consider changes in expected MFP to be expectations of *trend* changes that will affect *trend* GDP.

- LRAS, AS, and AD all shift in the same direction in response to an MFP shock.

- We will assume that firms immediately recognize the supply shock and adjust wages, prices, employment, and output to the new Long-Run equilibrium level; there are no inventory or labor market adjustments and we immediately move to Long-Run equilibrium in both the goods and labor markets.

11.3.1 Example: An Exogenous Increase in Expected MFP

Aggregate Demand Effects

Aggregate Demand will shift to the right in response to an increase in expected Multi-Factor Productivity:

- Households expect their lifetime incomes to increase and so they increase their Consumption accordingly.

- The marginal productivity of capital increases at any level of Investment, shifting the domestic Investment demand curve to the right and resulting (regardless of the impact on world interest rates) in an increase in domestic Investment spending.

- If there are increased capital inflows to take advantage of our increased mpk, then the associated exchange-rate appreciation will cause the trade balance to fall, somewhat offsetting the positive influences on AD.

The total size of the AD shift will be affected by the size of the expenditure multiplier.

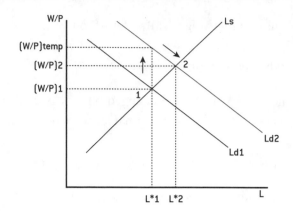

Labor Market Effects

Labor Demand will shift to the right as a result of the increase in expected Multi-Factor Productivity:

- The increase in Investment spending results in a higher equilibrium capital stock.

- The increase in MFP and in the capital stock jointly contribute to an increase in the marginal productivity of labor at any level of employment.

- Unless Labor Supply is backward-bending (see **Chapter 3**), firms will pay a higher real wage at the initial level of employment, but more than compensating workers for the value of their leisure. Workers will enter the labor market, driving down the marginal productivity of labor and the real wage to a new equilibrium at a higher level of employment (**Figure 4**).

Aggregate Supply Effects

The AS and LRAS curves shift to the right:

- The rightward shift in the Labor Demand curve corresponds to a rightward shift in Aggregate Supply.

- All three equilibrium inputs (MFP, K, and L) are higher, resulting in a rightward shift of the LRAS curve and an increase in potential (trend) GDP.

Equilibrium

The movement to a new goods market equilibrium is shown in **Figure 5**:

- The impact on nominal Wages and Prices is ambiguous—it depends on the size of the AS and AD shifts.

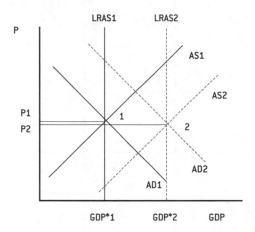

- The real wage increases unambiguously with the rise in the productivity of labor.

- Employment increases unless income effects compensate for substitution effects in the labor market (i.e. so long as Labor Supply is upward-sloping).

- Output increases and real Aggregate Demand increases in equilibrium.

PRACTICE PROBLEMS

1. Assume that the U.S. economy starts from a long-run equilibrium in both the goods and labor markets and show this situation graphically. Graph the impact of a decrease in U.S. government expenditures on the goods and labor markets and make reference to your graphs as you explain how the economy will adjust to a new long-run equilibrium.

SUGGESTED ANSWERS

1. AD falls. At P1, AD<AS and so inventories accumulate. Firms realize they want to cut production and so they reduce L input. As L falls, mpl rises from diminishing returns. Under perfect competition, w/p=mpl and so real wages rise as well and we move along Ld to point 2.

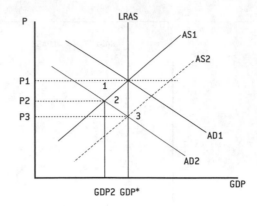

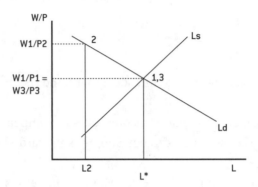

Assuming that nominal wages are unable to adjust immediately (nominal wages constant), the rise in the real wage means that the Price level must be falling. Thus P falls as GDP falls and we move along AS to point 2.

As Prices fall, AD increases because of any or all of the reasons why AD is downward-sloping—the international substitution effect, the real wealth effect, or the inter-temporal substitution effect.

Point 2 is a goods market equilibrium but it is not a labor market equilibrium: unemployed workers bid down the nominal wage, which makes them more attractive to firms. As L increases, mpl falls (diminishing returns) and w/p fall (as w falls, but also because w/p=mpl). The labor market continues to adjust until real wages fall to their original level and L returns to L* at point 3 (same as point 1).

As Wages fall, costs fall at any level of output, and so firms must (under perfect competition) charge a lower Price at any level of output: AS shifts down. As wages and prices fall, we move along AD again to return to GDP* at a lower price, lower wages, original real wages, and the original level of employment at point 3.

FISCAL POLICY

Fiscal policy includes all spending and taxation decisions by federal, state, and local governments. Most spending decisions by all levels of government are for long-term projects and programs (such as roads and schools and government-sponsored health care), but other types of spending are more cyclical in nature. Some types of spending increase automatically during recessions (such as unemployment insurance and welfare payments), but spending also changes over the business cycle as a result of policy—in order to try to reverse the course of the business cycle. We will talk about long-term and cyclical changes in spending and taxation in this chapter, as well as the impact of fiscal spending and taxation decisions on the rest of economy using the model we've developed through **Chapter 11** of this text.

12.1 SOURCES AND ALLOCATIONS OF GOVERNMENT RESOURCES

Fiscal spending is broken down into two categories in our model and in the U.S. data:

- *Government Expenditures* are direct spending on goods and services by federal, state, and local governments; in our National Income Accounting framework these are recorded as Government Expenditures.

- *Transfers* are allocations of money to households and firms; spending by households is recorded as Consumption Expenditures, spending by firms as Investment Expenditures.

12.1.1 Government Expenditures

Government Expenditures includes spending on infrastructure (transportation, utilities, postal services, telecommunications, sanitation, and so on) that are also offered, in many countries, by private enterprise. This type of fiscal spending comes under the heading "Government Expenditures" in the Aggregate Expenditures approach to national income accounting, rather than under the heading "Investment" because although the spending may be an input into production efficiency, the spending decisions by Government are not driven by the same economic considerations as are spending decisions by firms.

In our introductory model, we will exclude this type of "government capital" from our production function (Government Expenditures do not contribute to the capital stock K), but other economic models sometimes disentangle this type of Government purchase from total fiscal expenditures and treat it as a type of capital input.

Government Expenditures also includes investments in human capital, such as public schooling, medical care, disease control, and so on. As suggested earlier, many of these services are also provided by private institutions. In either case, the contribution to human capital offered by these services to labor productivity is reflected in the real wage.

In the United States the two largest categories of Government Expenditures are defense expenditures and interest payments on the large Federal government debt.

12.1.2 Transfers

Government Transfers to *firms* sometimes take the form of subsidies to firm Investments; in those cases, the government is playing a role in the market for loans that private enterprise could have played. In some cases, the Government Transfer is designed to correct a *market failure* that would have resulted in too little Investment from the perspective of national welfare. In other cases the subsidy is purely "pork" spending.[1] Naturally, every firm looking for a government subsidy argues that they fit in the latter category, whereas critics of the subsidy will argue it is simply "pork."

Government Transfers to *households* include student loan subsidies, food stamps, aid to families with dependent children, Social Security (federal old age and retirement), unemployment benefits, Medicare (old-age health care) and Medicaid (health care for the poor), tax rebates, and so on. They are transfers of money that affect household lifetime disposable income and therefore also Consumption (and Savings) decisions.

Figure 1 shows a breakdown of U.S. Fiscal spending by Expenditure Category; the chart includes both Government Expenditures and Government Transfers.

12.1.3 Government Revenue

Government revenue is earned through taxation. The sources of U.S. Federal tax revenue are shown in **Figure 2**.

One type of taxation that is often in the news is the *capital gains tax*. The capital gains tax is the tax paid on income earned from asset ownership (stocks, bonds, houses, and so on). One reason the capital gains tax is controversial is that it reduces the return on lending, which discourages lending and therefore reduces aggregate Investment in capital goods. Most economists agree that it would be better for the Government to raise money in some way that does not discourage Investment; what they do not agree on is what the other way might be!

---

[1]The term "pork barrel spending" refers to the practice of giving something—historically pork from a barrel—in exchange for votes.

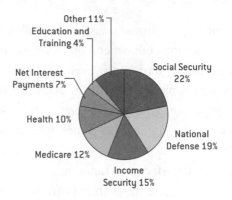

12.1.3.1 Lump-Sum Taxes

If the Government were to tax each household the same amount of money, regardless of that household's income, then that would be what economists call a "lump-sum tax." We do not have lump-sum taxation in the U.S. because it is considered regressive. (A regressive tax is one that hurts the poor more than it hurts the rich; lump sum taxes are considered regressive because they take away a larger fraction of the income of poor households.) However, lump-sum taxation is a very easy way to describe taxation in introductory models of the macroeconomy, and so we sometimes refer to it in this text even though it is not generally observed in the real world.

12.1.4 Fiscal Spending and Taxation Over the Business Cycle

A *counter-cyclical* fiscal policy would offset swings in other components of Aggregate Expenditures with equal-and-opposite swings in Government Expenditures (thus ending the recession or boom in Aggregate spending). Government Expenditures are not very cyclical, partly because of the nature of the spending (defense, interest payments, and long-term spending on roads and schools and so on), and partly because it is difficult for Congress to

FIGURE 2: SHARE OF U.S. FEDERAL TAX REVENUE FROM VARIOUS CATEGORIES (2003)

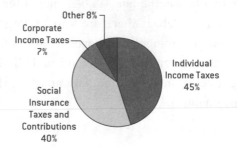

approve and implement new spending programs quickly enough to "counter" U.S. business cycles.

Unlike Government Expenditures, transfers and taxation *are* very cyclical. In part, this is because Transfers and Taxation both depend on income earned by households, and so they automatically rise and fall during business cycles. Transfers automatically rise during economic downturns because more people are eligible for unemployment benefits and other forms of welfare, and because more people choose to enter retirement. More taxation automatically falls during economic downturns as aggregate incomes fall because so much tax revenue is earned through income taxes.

Automatic changes in Transfers and Taxation are not the only reason that they tend to move with the business cycle. Congress tends to approve increases in Transfers (extension of unemployment benefits, for example) during downturns and at the same time to approve cuts in taxation, in order to try to quickly "stimulate" household and firm spending in a counter-cyclical way. These *counter-cyclical* fiscal policies tend to get passed through Congress in a timely enough way that they have potential impact on economic activity—potentially helping the economy recover more quickly from recession. As we will see, however, even the efficacy of these counter-cyclical policies is far from clear because of the negative impact on the economy of any increase in Government Borrowing (as revenues fall and spending increases).

12.1.5 Government Borrowing

12.1.5.1 The Government Budget Deficit

Governments, like households, can borrow money in periods in which spending exceeds revenues, and save in periods in which revenues exceed spending. If a government is borrowing in any time period, then we say it is running a *government budget deficit* (there is more money leaving government coffers than is entering); if the government is saving in any time period, then we say that it is running a *budget surplus* (more money entering than leaving government accounts).

In 2001 the Federal Government accrued the largest fiscal deficit in U.S. history; this is daunting, but we must keep in mind that the U.S. economy has also been growing over time—it was not the largest deficit as a share of GDP.

12.1.5.2 Government Budget Debt

Debt is defined as the sum total of all outstanding loans; the U.S. government debt is the stock (sum) of all the previous deficits and surpluses. The U.S. government has been adding to its debt in all but a few quarters in the late 1990s, when it temporarily ran a surplus. Not surprisingly, the U.S. government debt is therefore a much larger share of GDP than is the deficit. Fortunately, the federal government will never be asked to pay all of that debt back at once! However, there is rising concern that the size of the U.S. debt is getting too large, and that its very magnitude might be having a detrimental impact on U.S. and world economic growth (as discussed later in the chapter).

Consider a temporary downturn caused by a fall in Investment spending that is not correlated with an (actual) fall in MFP. In that case, AD falls below GDP*, and unplanned inventory accumulation leads to a fall in employment, production, and prices in the way described in **Chapter 11**. This type of cyclical downturn is shown in **Figure 3**.

Eventually, wages and labor markets will adjust to bring the economy back to equilibrium at a lower Price level, but this may take a long time. Fiscal policymakers may instead try to counter the fall in Investment Spending with an increase in Government Spending; this would hypothetically increase AD and return the economy to potential GDP without having to wait for the labor market to adjust.

Other counter-cyclical fiscal policies that could be used might be to either increase transfers (welfare) or to cut taxes—in either case, households and firms would ideally increase their expenditures and, again, AD would return to its original level.

Obviously, things are not so simple, or governments would always do this and we would never have lengthy recessions or periods of unemployment! One reason that fiscal policy-makers do not automatically "counter" any change in Aggregate Demand with increases (or decreases) in spending has already been alluded to—it is difficult for Congress to agree on where they would like to *allocate* the spending, and so by the time they respond to the economic downturn it is "too late" in the sense that labor markets are already adjusting and the economy is already in recovery.

Another reason that fiscal policy may have a limited effect on Aggregate Demand has to do with the implications of the policy for the government budget, and the indirect effects that the U.S. budget deficit has on the rest of the economy.

FIGURE 3:

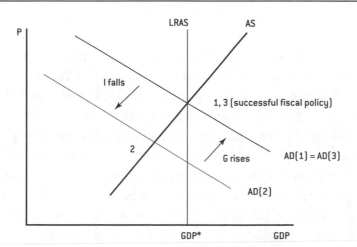

12.2.1 Rationality and the Implications for Counter-Cyclical Fiscal Policy

Consider again the scenario in **Figure 3**: AD falls, and fiscal policymakers respond by increasing Government Spending. The direct effect of the counter-cylical policy is to increase AD and return it back toward its original level. However, the increase in Government spending also results in an increase in the U.S. government budget deficit, and rational households know that the only way to pay off this increase in the debt will be to either increase taxes later on, or to decrease spending later on, so that future surpluses can pay off the current borrowing. In either case, rational households know that their future disposable income will be lower, which means that their expected lifetime disposable income is falling. Rational households will cut current Consumption at the same time that Government spending is increasing!

In other words, if households are rational (and not credit constrained), then they will save exactly enough today that they need to pay off the future tax increase, which means that they will save exactly the same amount that is being borrowed. C falls by the same amount that G increases, and there is no impact on AD. [Note these things happen simultaneously, so there is no temporary positive income effect on AD.]

To be even more precise, rationality (without credit constraints) implies that it doesn't make any difference when the Government pays for fiscal spending increases—paying today or tomorrow is *equivalent* in terms of the impact on Aggregate Demand. This description of the inefficacy of counter-cylical fiscal policy is known as *Barro-Ricardo Equivalence*.

Barro-Ricardo Equivalence implies that fiscal policies are useless in affecting AD! However, the result relies on (at least) two very strict assumptions: that all households are perfectly rational, and that no households are credit-constrained. What do the data say on the subject? As always, it is hard to tell because there are so many things influencing spending behavior, but the 2000 recession does give us some insight into the question.

Recent Evidence

Congress became concerned in the Spring of 2001 that the economy might be sliding into recession; it enacted a series of tax cuts and approved a tax rebate for that summer to reimburse people for some of the taxes they'd already paid that year. The rebate applied only to taxpayers (it excluded the very poor and unemployed) and was a lump-sum payment of $300 per eligible person. The rebate was designed to immediately stimulate Consumer spending and help keep the economy out of recession. At the same time, the tax cut and rebate helped move the U.S. government budget from a position of surplus to one of deficit.

Unfortunately, the tax rebates of 2001 had only a very small impact on Consumer spending, and it was estimated that households *saved* at least 3/4 of the rebate. This experience might suggest that, during times of recession at any rate, households indeed are very rational. Households may have suspected that the tax rebate and tax cuts had no implication for their lifetime tax bill, and so they saved the rebate either for future tax increases or for future income decreases (because they were worried about the recession getting worse).

The example does not end there, however. In 2003 Congress approved a *second* set of tax rebates, affiliated with deeper cuts in taxes and an even larger budget deficit. This time, households *did* spend the majority of the tax rebates! The difference in response to the tax rebate later in the economic downturn could be interpreted either as evidence that credit constraints became important as the downturn dragged on or as evidence against rationality.

12.2.2 The Relationship Between Government Deficits and Trade Deficits

If households are perfectly rational and have no credit constraints, then any increase in Government borrowing is exactly matched by an increase in Household Savings—households save more because their lifetime disposable incomes are reduced by the expected future tax increase.

In terms of our National Income Accounting equation, the previous paragraph can be summarized as follows:

$$S - I = \text{Household Savings} + \text{Public Sector Savings} - I = X - M$$

$$S - I = \text{Household Savings} (\uparrow) + \text{Public Sector Savings} (\downarrow) - I = X - M = \text{unchanged}$$

If households are rational (and not credit constrained), the increase in public sector borrowing (fall in public sector savings) has no impact on total U.S. Savings and therefore no impact on international capital flows or on world loan scarcity or on the U.S. trade balance.

What if households are either irrational or credit constrained? Then the fall in Public Sector Savings is *not* offset by Household behavior and total domestic Savings falls. The fall in U.S. total Savings may not be large enough to affect world loan scarcity, in which case world interest rates and Investment levels are unaffected, but the increase in the U.S. capital account surplus (borrowing from foreigners to finance our budget deficit) results in an increase in the demand for dollars, appreciation of the dollar, and a reduction in our trade balance.

$$(S - I) \downarrow = (X - M) \downarrow$$

Government is stimulating the economy on the one hand (through increased Government expenditures or Transfers), but the negative impact on the trade balance is at least partially offsetting the stimulative effect on Aggregate Demand!

Therefore even if people are irrational, there will a negative indirect effect on Aggregate Demand of any deficit-financed government policy. This negative effect is often referred to as the *twin deficits* relationship—the twin of a government budget deficit may be a trade deficit.

12.2.3 Does Government Borrowing Crowd Out Private Investment?

In the previous example, it was assumed that the Government budget deficit was too small to affect world interest rates. This clearly depends on the size of the borrowing! If the

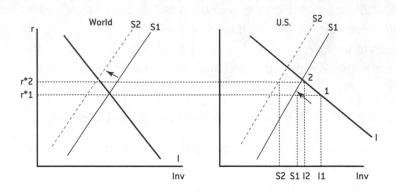

Government deficit is large enough to affect world loan scarcity, then under perfect competition higher world real interest rates will force firms to earn higher returns on their Investments; firms will cut back on Investment spending, which will raise the marginal productivity of capital until U.S. and world Investment levels reach a new, lower equilibrium level. This situation is known as "crowding out"—in which government borrowing, by competing with firms for access to a limited supply of loans, causes Investment to fall. This situation is shown graphically in **Figure 4,** assuming the U.S. starts out in capital account surplus. (The description of how we move to equilibrium is omitted, but you might work through it as review on your own!)

Note that there are two critical assumptions for crowding out to take place: households must be either irrational or credit constrained, and the budget deficit must be large enough to affect world loan scarcity. In this case, any stimulative effect of the counter-cyclical fiscal policy will be partially offset by a decrease in *Investment* spending (perhaps as well as a decrease in the trade balance).

PRACTICE PROBLEMS

1. Show the U.S. and world markets for capital under the assumption that the U.S. is in a capital account surplus. For this example, assume that the U.S. is too small to affect world interest rates and households follow a rule of thumb in their spending decisions. Graph the impact of an increase in the U.S. Government expenditures with no increase in current taxation. Show the impact on the U.S. capital account and explain what is going on in your graph.

2. Graph the market for the U.S. dollar in terms of Yen. Based on your answer to Part 1, graph the impact of a deficit-financed increase in U.S. Government spending on the value of the dollar in terms of Yen as well as on the U.S. trade balance. Explain what is going on in your graph.

3. What is the total impact on Aggregate Demand of the increase in Government spending? Is there crowding out in the example? Why or why not?

SUGGESTED ANSWERS

1. Public Savings falls as Government Spending increases while government income remains unchanged. The U.S. Savings curve shifts to the left. There is no change in world interest rates because the U.S. is assumed to be too small to affect world loan scarcity. Therefore S falls but I remains unchanged: S-I falls and the capital account moves farther into surplus.

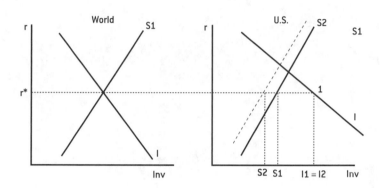

2. If foreigners are lending more to the U.S., then they need more dollars in order to do so. Demand for dollars increases as demand for U.S. assets increases (government bonds are the asset demanded in this case). D>S of dollars at the old exchange rate, and so the dollar appreciates. As the exchange rate rises, Exports fall (cost more to foreigners) and U.S. Imports rise (foreign goods seem cheaper to the U.S.), and the trade balance goes further into deficit.

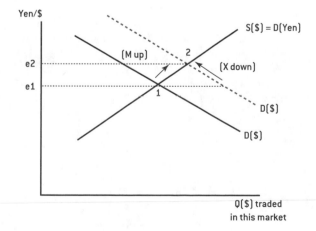

3. Going through each AD component to see that AD increases but the increase in G is off-set somewhat by a decline in the trade balance:

   a. C is unchanged (except through the multiplier effect) because households don't change their savings in anticipation of future tax increase.

   b. I is unchanged because world real interest rates are unaffected. There is no crowding out because government spending doesn't affect world interest rates in this example.

   c. G increases.

   d. X-M falls.

MONEY

In our model economy, all economic decisions are made in real terms, yet nominal variables (prices) adjust to bring supply and demand for goods and services into equilibrium. In modern economies those prices are almost always denominated in terms of money. Because the existence and qualities of money are so fundamental to modern economies, we'll spend some time in this chapter discussing its origins and properties. We'll start by considering the monetary system's alternative means of conducting trade: barter (the trade of a set of goods or services for another).

Barter arrangements continue to exist today between nations (weapons for oil, food for peace, bilateral trade agreements, and so on), between firms (patent-sharing, exchanging celebrity product endorsement with supplies of the product itself, etc), and between individuals ("you wash, I'll dry" and other, sometimes more formal, arrangements).

Now, in our model, and arguably in the world around us, the only way to get something is to produce something—all money income is ultimately the result of work. One might then ask why we use money at all. Why not just barter? This type of questioning may lead one next to wonder whether the use of money rather than barter affects things in the economy in any important ways, and, if so, how.

13.1 WHY NOT JUST BARTER?

13.1.1 Barter Requires a Double Coincidence of Wants

One problem with barter is that it requires what economists clumsily call a *double coincidence of wants* between the two trading partners—you have to want what I have to offer, and I simultaneously (*coincidentally*) have to want what you have to offer. In a primitive economy, most everyone is producing a good that satisfies a basic need (something that everyone wants), and so barter trades can be a market-clearing mechanism because everyone is producing something everyone else wants. So, for example, if your neighbor owns a well and produces fresh water and you raise cattle, then the neighbor can provide water to you in exchange for a certain amount of beef.

In lieu of a double coincidence of wants, barter becomes risky. Imagine that there are three commodities in the economy: well supplies, beef, and water. You need water to care for your cattle, the owner of the well needs supplies, and the producer of well supplies wants beef. In that case, there is no double coincidence of wants. You might be tempted to trade beef for well supplies, and then approach the owner of the well for that trade. But if you did so, the owner of the well would have you over a barrel (so to speak!)—she knows that you are stuck with well supplies from which you derive no utility and which you cannot sell to anyone else. So she will offer you a rock-bottom price (in terms of water) and you will get very little water for your cattle. Of course, if this happens to you even once then you will not try it again, and the whole trading system will fall apart: there is no barter without double coincidence of wants.

13.1.2 Too Many Prices

Imagine an economy with two products: snake oil and apples. There will exist a market-clearing price for apples in terms of snake oil (pints per apple, for example) that is based purely on barter between snake oil and apple producers. Now imagine a third product—oranges—is introduced into the economy. Now apples have at least two prices: one in terms of snake oil, one in terms of oranges. If oranges or snake oil are durable (last more than the period it takes to trade them), then there is at least one more price for apples that is a certain number of oranges in combination with a certain amount of snake oil. And of course snake oil also has at least two prices and so do oranges. As the number of goods in the economy grows, the number of prices grows even faster.

If, however, all goods are denominated in terms of units of currency, then each good has exactly one price. Money is a *unit of account* that improves the transparency of the value of trades—if I sell snake oil to an apple farmer, I can easily work out what the purchasing power of that sale is in terms of the other goods and services I will eventually get in the market.

13.1.3 Divisibility and Barter

There are divisibility problems with many barter arrangements—if the market-clearing exchange between a doctor and a rancher is one-and-a-half cows per tonsillectomy, then one of them needs to find a buyer for the other half of a cow; if they are unable to find such a buyer, then the effective price is two cows per tonsillectomy, which is not a market-clearing price.

Historically, people in primitive societies often got around the divisibility problem by adding a third commodity to their exchange prices. That third commodity would be something one of the traders had acquired in a previous exchange, and it would usually be something of low value whose quantity could be adjusted to bring the total barter payment to the market-clearing level. One such commonly-used commodity in many primitive economies was wheat—quantities were easily adjusted to match any market price, it was in general demand as a consumption-good and was therefore useful in many transactions, and it was storable, which meant that, once acquired, it could be saved for future trades.

Indeed, wheat assumed the role of an early form of money in many primitive societies as more and more large-scale payments and transactions were denominated in amounts of wheat, with credits and debits from "wheat banks" recorded as payment for these transactions. Thus wheat can be considered money in some circumstances but not others! The next section defines the qualities embodied by anything that can be called "money."

13.2 WHAT WE MEAN BY "MONEY"

Money is defined as something that embodies the following three properties:

- It is a medium of exchange (it serves a market-clearing role between buyers and sellers of goods and services)

- It is a unit of account (it can be used to value all goods and services in the economy)

- It is a store of value (if received in a transaction, it need not immediately be either consumed or traded but can be used in future time periods)

In the previous section, wheat came to take on the properties of money because it satisfied all three of these requirements. Obviously that is no longer the case! Objects that currently pass for money may not always do so. So, for example, during the interwar period, rapid inflation of the German Reichsmark sufficiently ate away at that currency's store of value (future purchasing power) that workers, shopkeepers, and others stopped accepting the currency in exchange for goods and services and, in many cases, reverted to direct barter, or to the use of *commodity* monies like gold or cigarettes to clear market transactions.

The different types of money that exist or have existed over time can be grouped into four categories: Commodity Money, Convertible Currency, Fiat Money, and Deposit Money.

13.2.1 Commodity Money

Section 13.1.3 discussed the use of a "third commodity" in barter trades that could be used to add to a barter exchange price between the traders of two different goods. A commodity money system is one in which all goods and services can be exclusively priced in terms of such a commodity. The commodity is "money" if it can be used as a means of payment, is a unit of account for all goods and services, and if it can be saved for future transactions (store of value). Barter systems themselves are not commodity money systems because no single good can be used to price all other goods and services.

There are various historical examples of commodity money systems, though in most cases they co-existed with barter trade. What differentiates commodity monies from other types of money is that the commodity itself can offer utility as a consumption good should the commodity lose any of the three qualities that make it useful as money. So, for example, a merchant in ancient Egypt that had accumulated wealth in the form of wheat—an early commodity money—didn't need to worry about whether wheat would continue to serve a role as money for the indefinite future because he could always consume the wheat himself or find someone else to barter with that would like to consume wheat products. One characteristic of commodity monies therefore is that they have a store of value as *consumption* goods.

Commodity monies used in U.S. history include *wampum*, gold, and cigarettes. In the 17th century, strings of wampum beads (mollusk shells with holes drilled through them) were legal tender in the U.S. and Canadian colonies. They were used for trades between the colonists and the native American Indian populations, but also for trades among the settlers. The *wampum* served ceremonial purposes among the native populations, and so were a type of commodity money for them; for the settlers, they maintained their store of value because they were also convertible at official exchange rates into European currency. *Wampum* was the first recorded currency to originate in the North American colonies.

Gold dust was used for trades throughout the U.S. well into the 19th century, but was quickly replaced by convertible currency (see below) for reasons of safety as well as because of the large transportation costs associated with large (heavy) gold payments.

Cigarettes were a commodity used in German P.O.W. camps during World War II. American soldiers received Reichsmark "salaries" while prisoners of war, and that currency was used to purchase supplies, through official channels (usually!), from local farmers and merchants. Soldiers in many camps however used cigarettes to clear trades *within* the camps—saving their Reichsmarks for trades outside the camp. Red Cross packages as well as food and goods sent from home to the P.O.W.s were traded through a centralized market in each camp and priced in terms of cigarettes.

13.2.1.1 Gresham's Law

Gresham's Law is the prediction that the inferior type of consumption good will always be the one used as the commodity money. Gresham's Law has some intuitive appeal: if it costs ten cigarettes to buy a certain product, it is better to use as payment the cigarettes that offer you the least utility as consumption goods because they have the lowest opportunity cost in terms of utility foregone.

13.2.1.2 Problems with Commodity Monies

One common problem with commodity money is that of *clipping*: merchants, or anyone else handling the commodity money, might surreptitiously take a "cut" and thereby reduce the commodity value of the gold bar or coin offered.

A second problem with commodity money is *debasement*. In the case of cigarette money, grass might be rolled in with the tobacco (this led to the acceptance of only pre-rolled, manufactured cigarettes such as Lucky Strikes, which could not have been altered by the trader). There were similar problems with metal coinage: Governments would mix inferior metals in with the gold and silver coins before paying their debts, thus effectively reducing the cost of the payments (this led to the practice of biting the coin to make sure that it was as soft as gold).

A third problem with commodity monies is that instability in the commodity value of the money may bleed through to economy-wide price instability. A drought, for example, that affects the commodity value of wheat could affect the in-terms-of-wheat price of every other good in a monetary system using wheat as currency.

13.2.2 Convertible Currency

Convertible Currencies are pieces of paper that are claims on particular amounts of a certain commodity. Convertible currency systems naturally evolved from commodity money systems as a means for reducing the transportation, security, and verification costs mentioned in **Section 13.2.1.** Goldsmiths offered the service of safely storing individual gold holdings and were also qualified to assay the value of the gold deposits on hand; in return the goldsmith would offer a receipt of the deposit made. Gold deposit receipts could then be signed over as means of payment, transferring ownership of shares of the gold from buyer to seller. When accepting payment, the seller receiving the gold claim need only trust the integrity of the goldsmith, rather than know anything about the credentials of the buyer or about how to assay the quality of the gold offered.

13.2.2.1 Problems with Convertible Currencies

Convertible currency systems are only stable so long as the utility derived from the commodity backing the system is expected to remain stable; variation in the utility value of the commodity backing the currency can, as in the commodity money system, undermine the monetary system.

A second source of uncertainty in convertible currency systems is the rate at which the paper currency is converted into the commodity. In the convertible currency system described in **Section 13.2.2**, deposit receipts were fully backed by gold, but that was not always the case. The U.S. dollar, for example, was, from 1945–1972, convertible at the rate of $35 per ounce of gold. That conversion rate was a non-market, or *fiat*, rate set by the U.S. government. Because the conversion rate was chosen by the government rather than the marketplace, it was plausible that the U.S. could change the conversion rate at any time; that uncertainty about the conversion rate eventually led to general price instability as people began to speculate on the market value of gold (and, by implication, on the market value of the dollar). In fact, in 1972, as the commodity value of gold skyrocketed, the U.S. abandoned backing of the dollar by gold, effectively instituting a new conversion rate of "zero ounces of gold per U.S. dollar." The U.S. dollar was then backed by, or convertible into, nothing at all! A currency that is not a commodity or is not convertible into a commodity is known as *fiat money*.

13.2.3 Fiat Money

Fiat money is paper money (or coin) that has no intrinsic value—it is acceptable as a means of payment only because we all agree to do so. The U.S. dollar is now fiat money and differs from Monopoly money only because users of dollars have agreed to give the patent of currency production to the federal government and to no one else. In fact, some other countries (Panama and, more recently, Ecuador, for example) have also decided to leave their currency production to the U.S. federal government and dollars function as fiat currency there as well.

When one stops to think about it, the whole concept is fairly remarkable! It relies on a coordination of beliefs—I must believe that everyone else in the marketplace will also believe that everyone else in the marketplace will accept fiat currency as payment before I will accept fiat currency as payment. If the system falls apart, then all wealth is lost and my currency holdings are not worth the paper they are printed on.

13.2.3.1 Problems with Fiat Money

One problem with the use of fiat money is that if people begin to *speculate* that the system will fall apart, then it *will* fall part. Expectations are self-fulfilling in the fiat money system: If people expect it to work it will work, but if people expect it to collapse then it will collapse.

A second problem with the use of fiat money is that it can be highly inflationary: holding potential output constant, more money just means higher prices. Because the fiat currency is not backed by any commodity, there is no limit to the amount that can be produced. (Note this is also an issue for the Convertible Currency system if the conversion rate is set by fiat.) As we'll discuss in **Chapter 14**, over-printing of currency leads to inflation, which eats away at the store of value of the currency; a hyperinflationary currency has no store of value and will cease to function as money. Consequently, fiat money systems only work if there is a central monetary authority that responsibly controls the money supply.

13.2.3.2 Safeguarding the U.S. Fiat Money System

Because one of the greatest threats to the fiat money system is inflation, the United States has set up a system designed to keep growth in the money supply under control. If the federal or state and local governments had authority to print currency, for example, then it would be very tempting for them to print out money with which to pay their bills, so that the cost of their debts would just be the cost of making money! The democratic system would eventually put such irresponsible governments out of work, but in the meantime there could be substantial damage to the economy.

The U.S. monetary authority that is responsible for deciding how much fiat money should be in circulation is known as the *Federal Reserve System*. The Federal Reserve System is designed to represent the interests of private enterprise and policy-makers, but also to constrain the interests of both parties. The Federal Reserve System consists of twelve regional Federal Reserve Banks that are overseen by the Federal Reserve Board (located in Washington, D.C.). The "governors" that sit on the Federal Reserve Board in Washington, together with the heads of the regional Banks, jointly make monetary policy decisions. The policy-making team, known as the Federal Open Market Committee or FOMC, is a mix of government appointees (the Governors of the Board are nominated by the President and approved by Congress) and privately-elected heads of the regional Banks. These regional Federal Reserve Banks are profit-making institutions with no incentive to bail out the government by printing money to pay its debts. Their operations, at the same time, are overseen by the Federal Reserve Board, which is a government enterprise.

Although the members of the Board of Governors are appointed by Congress and the President, they serve much longer terms than the politicians that appoint them (14 years), and so they are not subject to the whims and pressures of the electoral process the way other government officials are.

None of the members of the FOMC are allowed to own assets that would allow them to benefit from any monetary policy decision they might make, and twice a year the head of the Board of Governors (the Chairman of the Federal Reserve Board) must report to Congress the reasons for the monetary decisions they have been making over the year.

Once the FOMC has made a decision about the money supply, the U.S. Treasury is in charge of producing the necessary currency. Production of dollars must be carefully managed to make counterfeiting of the currency as difficult as possible; sufficient supplies of counterfeit money would be inflationary and undermine the U.S. payments system.

13.2.4 Deposit Money

Deposit money has no physical currency but is nevertheless a means of payment, unit of account, and store of value—it is the fourth type of money. U.S. checking deposits are an example of deposit money: they are a unit of account that does not depend on how the wealth was accumulated or how it will be spent, they are a means of payment because checks can be drawn against them, and they are a store of value because they can be used in future periods but also because they often offer interest payments that compensate for the depreciative effect of inflation on the purchasing power of the deposit money.

As increasingly more transactions are made using debit cards and other electronic means of payment, there is growing speculation that the use of paper and coin may one day be a thing of the past. However, deposit money in the United States is currently convertible into fiat money (paper currency and coin), and fiat and deposit monies together make up the total U.S. money supply.

13.2.4.1 Problems with Deposit Money

Like fiat money, deposits only function as money so long as traders maintain their faith and confidence that the system will continue. In the case of deposit money, that translates into faith and confidence in the banking system: because wealth and income have no physical representation, employees, landlords, doctors, lawyers, and so on must all have confidence that their accounts are managed correctly and that sufficient safeguards are in place to guarantee that neither human nor computer error could erode the store of value of deposit money holdings of wealth.

13.2.4.2 Safeguarding the U.S. Deposit Money System

The U.S. money supply is a mix of fiat and deposit monies. Because the U.S. Federal Reserve System is concerned with the total money supply, it is also concerned about bank behavior, and the creation of deposit monies. The Federal Reserve contributes to the stability of the U.S. banking system in many ways, including:

- Provision of check-clearing services and fund transfers to and between member banks

- Safekeeping of reserves of fiat money needed to satisfy demands for conversion of deposit money into cash and coin

- Supervision and regulation of members of the banking system to ensure accurate and responsible management of deposits

Other responsibilities and operations of the Federal Reserve will be described in **Chapters 14** and **15**.

MONEY AND BANKING IN THE UNITED STATES

Banks play an important part in the U.S. monetary and payments system both because, as financial intermediaries, they facilitate the use of deposit money and also because they provide safe storage of fiat money (see **Chapter 13**). In order to understand more about the role of banks in affecting the economy, we need go into more detail about bank behavior.

14.1 LIQUIDITY OF FINANCIAL ASSETS

Banks in the U.S. play an important role in affecting both Consumption and Investment spending. Household savings allocated to banks is allocated to the market for loans, funding capital investments for firms and earning interest income to both bankers and depositors; that interest income helps maintain the store of value of the money saved by households, and so helps maintain the payments system. At the same time, savings deposited by households into the banking system is relatively *liquid* compared to putting savings into one's own firm, house, or the stock market.

The degree of *liquidity* of a financial asset refers to the ease with which savings can be converted into spending. Because liquidity is desirable, banks compete with each other to reduce the costs of converting different types of savings accounts back into a medium of exchange.

Generally, the less liquid the financial asset, the higher the rate of return needed to compensate savers for the transaction cost of changing the asset into a liquid form. So, for example, you cannot pay the rent by writing a draft onto a savings account; instead, you have first to transfer funds from your savings into a checking account. Savings accounts, on the other hand, offer higher rates of return than do checking accounts: Because they are less liquid, people are less likely to use them to buy goods and services, and so banks are able to lend out a fraction of the funds (paying interest) on the expectation that they will not be in demand.

Time deposit accounts are an even less liquid type of savings account that specify that the saver pays a *penalty* if the money is withdrawn before a specified time; that penalty reduces the liquidity of the asset. Banks are then able, on expectation, to allocate time deposit money to longer-term projects that offer a higher expected return; that higher return is shared with the depositor.

14.2 FOUR DEFINITIONS OF THE U.S. MONEY SUPPLY

One simple definition of the U.S. money supply is that it consists of the sum of fiat money and deposit money (see **Chapter 13**). Unfortunately, that definition is a bit too simplistic for practical application! So, for example, do we want to include all U.S. dollars or just those in the United States? If the latter, do we want to include dollars sitting in bank vaults, held in reserve for conversion of deposit money into cash, or would that lead to unwanted double-counting of some deposit monies? Which types of deposits should we include—only checking accounts or also savings and time deposits?

The answer is that one might include different types of financial assets in different circumstances. Because government agencies arrange the data so that they can be used by analysts and economists, they publish several different definitions of the U.S. money supply. One measure, M0, also known as the Monetary Base, includes only fiat money. The two most common measures include only the fiat money that is in circulation (i.e., it excludes bank reserves), plus some types of deposit money.

Until the 1980s, M1 was the most commonly-used definition of the U.S. money supply: M1 only includes things that can actually be used as a means of payment by firms and households in the economy; it excludes cash holdings that are sitting in bank vaults and are not therefore in circulation, and it excludes savings, time, and mutual fund deposits because, *at that time,* they could not be used as a means of payment.

In the 1980s, however, deregulation of the banking industry allowed banks to compete more directly with each in terms of the types of services they offered. At the same time, technological progress allowed for the introduction of new banking services such as automatic teller machines,

Money Definition	Currency in public circulation	Currency in bank reserves	Travellers' checks*	Checking deposits*	Savings deposits*	Time deposits[f]	Mutual fund deposits*
M0	X	X					
M1	X		X	X			
M2	X		X	X	X	X	X

*Held by private firms and individuals
[f]Excludes large-denomination time deposits

cash and debit cards, and so on. The result was the introduction of electronic means of banking that made it possible for firms and households to make some types of payments directly from their savings accounts, and to instantly move funds from time and mutual fund deposits *into* checking and savings accounts. Many economists therefore now prefer the broader money definition M2.

Critics of the use of M2 argue that while savings accounts are a means of payment, time and mutual fund deposits are not; it is still necessary to first convert those types of deposits into a means of payment before they can be used to buy goods and services and so they do not satisfy the "means of payment" requirement of money.

14.3 MONEY AND INFLATION: THE QUANTITY THEORY OF MONEY

One basis for the selection of a money definition is the reliability of the measure as a predictor of inflation. The logic behind the relationship between money and prices is quite intuitive. The quantity of goods and services is determined by potential long-run Aggregate Supply. The nominal *value* of long-run Aggregate Supply is equal to P*GDP. The more money in circulation, the higher the value of GDP can be, but all of that increase in the value of GDP comes from increases in prices (GDP is determined by MFP, K and L inputs, not by the quantity of money in circulation). *Assuming that potential GDP is not affected by the money supply*, doubling the amount of money should, all other things being equal, double prices.

In the real world, households and producers exchange many goods and services, and so the person receiving a $1 bill for an apple would then spend it on something else—that single dollar bill gets used many times in a month, quarter, year, or whatever time period is relevant. The more times it gets used, the more goods are bought. The value of the goods and services bought over the whole time period has to be equal to the amount of money in the economy *multiplied by the number of times the money is used*. The turnover of money, or the number of times it is used in a given time period, is known as the *velocity* of money.

The relationship between the value of things sold and the money supply is known as the *Quantity Theory of Money*. Algebraically, the Quantity Theory of Money (QTM) can be written

Money Supply * Velocity = Price Level * GDP,
where Velocity and GDP are exogenous with respect to Money

QTM is a *theory* of money, rather than a factual relationship, because of the conditions in the definition that follow the word "where." Those conditions imply that *any growth in the money supply is, all other things being equal, matched by an equal change in the price level (inflation)*. What's more, QTM implies that any change in the price level, holding velocity and GDP constant, must be the result of changes in the money supply. That is a strong result!

The assumption that money growth does not affect GDP is quite consistent with the model that we have been developing in class, in which all growth in GDP *ultimately* stems from population and MFP growth. The qualifier that GDP "ultimately" (in the long run) stems from growth in those two inputs is very important: the QTM is only used as a *long run* predictor of the relationship between money growth and inflation.

The second assumption behind QTM is that velocity, or the number of times money is used in a given time period, is exogenous with respect to the quantity of money in circulation.

That is not to say that velocity never changes: Velocity *is* affected by technological progress, the weather, tastes and preferences of consumers, and so on. Although velocity may change, we will assume that it is unaffected by money.

Now, policymakers and analysts that are trying to predict inflation will often use the Quantity Theory of Money (or fancy versions of it that carefully model a relationship between money growth, GDP, and velocity). They therefore choose the definition of money that gives the most stable (unchanging) estimate of the velocity of money; that definition is, not surprisingly, the *broader* definition of money: M2. The broader definition of money is naturally more stable because if people reallocate their money holdings across types of deposits, such as between savings and checking accounts, there will be no change in the velocity of M2 but the velocity of M1 might change a lot.

14.4 FRACTIONAL RESERVE BANKS AND THE ECONOMY

Banks take deposits and allocate them to borrowers in exchange for a fee. Not all of the deposit is lent in this manner: a *fraction* is held in *reserve* to meet the expected day-to-day checking (deposit money) and cash (fiat money) requirements of the bank's customers—hence these types of banks are known as *fractional reserve banks*.

14.4.1 Bank Runs

Imagine that you and I each deposit $100 in the same bank, and that the bank holds 50% of every deposit in reserve, lending out the rest. By doing so, the bank is gambling that the sum of our liquidity needs will be no more than $100. And of course, you and I are making the same gamble: if we both need all of our deposit back at the same time, the bank will be short $100. In that case, the smartest thing for each of us to do is to run as fast as we can to get our deposit back before the bank runs out of reserves.

In the real world, banks have many customers, but the logic is the same: if there is a widespread belief that the bank will run out of reserves, then customers will make a run on the bank and try to remove all of their deposits at once. The banking system is not set up to accommodate so much demand at one time, and so some customers will get all of their deposits in cash, while others farther down the line will get nothing and will have to wait until people start paying back loans. The catch is that if people can't get to their deposits, they can't pay off their loans, and so the whole system collapses: the people first in line win but everyone else loses. This is an illustration of the cost of a *bank run*.

Bank runs can only happen in fractional reserve banking systems, yet households usually are willing to take the risk in exchange for the interest they earn on their deposits; that interest in turn helps them to maintain the store of value of their wealth, and also helps them to avoid the costs of monitoring loans themselves (see **Chapter 7**).

In summary, the fractional reserve banking system, like the fiat and deposit money systems, works so long as everyone believes it will work.

14.4.2 Fractional Reserve Banks Affect the World Interest Rate

The equilibrium (real expected) world interest rate is determined by the intersection of world demand and world supply of loans. Household and Government Savings may be directly allocated to borrowers, or they may operate through financial intermediaries like banks. When a household puts savings in a bank, a fraction is held in reserve: the more that is held in reserve, the fewer loans are being made; the fewer loans that are being made, the scarcer are loans; the scarcer are loans, the higher are world interest rates. (Graphically, world Savings shifts to the left as banks increase the fraction of deposits held in reserve.)

14.4.3 Fractional Reserve Banks "Create" Money

Imagine that you find $100 under your mattress and put it in the bank, which then holds 50% of that deposit in reserve. The other $50 is lent out to a borrower, and the interest paid on that loan is shared between you and the bank. When the bank gives the borrower the $50 check, it is deposited and becomes part of that borrower's checking account. Checking accounts are part of M1 (and M2), and so by making the loan, the bank has *created* a deposit and has therefore *created* money! Fractional reserve banks create money by creating deposits every time they make a loan.

Banks generally follow a fairly simple rule of thumb: they hold a constant fraction of every deposit in reserve, and lend the rest out. Continuing the previous example, that implies that when the borrower deposited the $50 loan check, the bank held 50% of *that* in reserve and created another deposit in the form of a $25 loan. When that loan check is deposited, 50% of that is lent out, creating an additional $12.50 deposit, and so on. In other words, there is a *multiplied* effect on the money supply for every initial deposit made. The total increase in the money supply is *larger* if the reserve-to-deposit ratio is *smaller*, because that means that more deposits are being created. In other words: *The money multiplier rises as the reserve ratio falls.*

The money multiplier shows the total change in the money supply for a given initial (exogenous) change in deposits. Algebraically, the money multiplier is derived as follows:

$$\Delta M2 = \Delta \overline{M2} + (1 - rr)* \Delta \overline{M2} + (1 - rr)* (1 - rr)* \Delta \overline{M2} + (1 - rr)* (1 - rr)* (1 - rr)* \Delta \overline{M2} + \ldots$$

where $\Delta \overline{M2}$ is the exogenous change in deposits and rr is the fraction of deposits held in reserve (the *reserve ratio*). The expression can be rewritten as

$$\Delta M2 = (1 - rr)^0 * \Delta \overline{M2} + (1 - rr)^1 * \Delta \overline{M2} + (1 - rr)^2 * \Delta \overline{M2} + \ldots$$

And because $(1 - rr) < 1$, the right hand side can be rewritten (using a Taylor expansion)

$$\Delta M2 = \frac{1}{1 - (1 - rr)} * \Delta \overline{M2} = \frac{1}{rr} * \Delta \overline{M2}$$

where $\frac{1}{rr}$ is the money multiplier.

14.4.4 The Short Run Relationship Between Money and GDP

Fractional reserve banks create money because they create loans; those loans, in turn, are spent on goods and services. Bank lending therefore affects Aggregate Demand. As we know from previous chapters, shifts in Aggregate Demand have only a temporary effect on GDP. In fact, that temporary effect may be so fleeting that we cannot see it in the GDP data! Even if that is the case, Aggregate Demand shocks emanating from the banking sector still affect prices and wages in the long run, and that price and wage instability is of concern to economists and policymakers.

If, on the other hand, bank behavior *does* have a temporarily noticeable impact on GDP, then it is the role of the Federal Reserve System to initiate regulations that will help prevent business cycles emanating from the banking sector (see next). Moreover, it also means that *monetary policy* can be used through the banking system to help *counter* cycles that emanate from other sectors of the economy: that will be the subject of **Chapter 15**.

14.5 REGULATION OF FRACTIONAL RESERVE BANKS

The fractional reserve banking system functions only so long as people believe it will; if we all pull money out at the same time (there is a bank run), then the system collapses.

Depositors will lose confidence in the system if they believe that the loans that have been made with their deposits will not be repaid; the consequence of that fall in confidence is the same regardless of whether the depositors' expectations are correct. Banking supervision—appraisal and monitoring of bank loans—helps reassure depositors that their banks are behaving responsibly. At the same time, *deposit insurance* of up to $100,000 per deposit (offered by the Federal Deposit Insurance Corporation) provides a safety net should things turn sour.

The Federal Deposit Insurance Corporation (FDIC) and the U.S. Federal Reserve System appraise the quality of all loans made by U.S. banks, and assess the overall exposure to market risk of each bank. Here are a few examples of requirements that bank supervisors will check for:

- Banks must have a diversified loan portfolio so that they are not overly-sensitive to the economic conditions of any particular industry.

- Bank loan portfolios must have a diversified length in maturity so that the bank's portfolio is not over-sensitive to events in any one time period.

- Bank managers must earn part of their pay in the form of equity in (part ownership of) the bank in which they operate, so that they are personally affected by their lending decisions.

At the same time that regulators want to encourage responsible lending practices, they also want to ensure that there is sufficient liquidity available for consumers to meet their day-to-day purchasing needs. Toward that end, the U.S. Federal Reserve System sets a minimum *required reserve ratio* of reserves as a fraction of total deposits. Should that prove insufficient to meet reserve demand, and banks are caught short of reserves, they have two options:

- Banks can borrow from each other in the interbank market, known as the federal funds market. The equilibrium interest rate determined in that market is known as the *federal funds rate*, although it is a free market rate and is not directly affected by the Federal Reserve or by the U.S. government. Banks may borrow in the federal funds market for any reason.

- Banks can borrow from their regional Federal Reserve Bank. The interest rate charged is known as the *discount rate*. The discount rate is not a competitive market rate and is set by the Federal Open Market committee. Banks may only borrow from the regional Federal Reserve Bank if they have fallen below the required reserve ratio.

Penalties are imposed against banks that frequently borrow from the regional Federal Reserve Bank, and so they generally prefer to borrow from each other in the interbank market. Banks in dire circumstances however may not be able to get a loan in the federal funds market. For that reason, a Federal Reserve Bank is often referred to as a "lender of last resort."

PRACTICE PROBLEMS

1. What is included in M2?

2. Based on your answer to Question 1, what is the total effect of a decrease in the required reserve ratio on M2? Give a detailed explanation.

3. Use the equation for the Quantity Theory of Money and your answers to Parts 1 and 2 to explain how reducing the required reserve ratio might affect inflation.

SUGGESTED ANSWERS

1. M2 includes cash, traveller's checks, checking deposits, savings and time deposits.

2. If the required reserve ratio is lower, then banks may make more loans. That will increase the deposit multiplier (equal to 1/reserve ratio) and so there will be more money "created" and an increase in M2.

3. Quantity Theory of Money: M2 * Velocity = Price Level * GDP.

Assuming that velocity and GDP growth are not only exogenous with respect to changes in the money supply but also unchanging, then a lower required reserve ratio will increase M2 and increase inflation.

MONETARY POLICYMAKING IN THE UNITED STATES

U.S. monetary policymaking is conducted by the Federal Open Market Committee (FOMC) of the Federal Reserve System (the "Fed"). The Federal Reserve Chairman reports twice yearly to Congress on the success the Fed has achieved and hopes to achieve in reaching each of the following three policy goals:

- Low unemployment

- Stabile prices

- Stabile exchange rates

This chapter will present some specifics about the mechanics of monetary policy and the limitations of its effectiveness, but it can be quickly summarized as follows: The Fed can encourage banks to lend more, which may lower world interest rates and thereby stimulate Aggregate Demand in the short run, but doing so puts upward pressure on prices and that may put downward pressure on the value of the dollar (through Purchasing Power Parity). In other words, if the Fed tries too hard to achieve one policy goal it will miss at least one of the others.

The three policy goals thus force the Fed to take a conservative approach to stimulating the economy, and to take an equally conservative approach when fighting inflation or when trying to affect the market value of the currency.

The Fed has three policy tools, each of which works by affecting the behavior of fractional reserve banks. They are

- Changing the required reserve ratio

- Changing the discount rate

- Changing the target federal funds (interbank) rate

15.1 FED POLICY OPTION: CHANGING THE REQUIRED RESERVE RATIO

One regulatory rule imposed by the Fed is that for every deposit made, a certain fraction is held in reserve. Banks prefer to hold as little in reserve as they can get away with, partly because providing security for reserves is expensive, but also because reserves do not earn interest. To reduce security costs banks may leave some of their reserve deposits at their regional Federal Reserve Bank, but they earn no interest on those deposits even if the Fed uses them to make loans (this is one way that the regional Federal Reserve Banks cover their operating costs).

15.1.1 Increasing the Required Reserve Ratio

If the required reserve ratio is increased, then banks must make fewer loans and hold more in reserve. Greater loan scarcity puts upward pressure on world interest rates and puts downward pressure on Aggregate Demand and therefore also on Prices. Moreover, as banks make fewer loans in the world market, their demand for foreign currency falls, and so foreign currencies depreciate relative to the dollar: U.S. imports rise and exports fall, putting further downward pressure on Aggregate Demand. [Note: an alternative explanation of events in the foreign exchange market would be that U.S. rates of return look temporarily attractive to foreigners, driving up demand for the dollar along with its price; either explanation would be acceptable.)

This policy might be chosen if the Fed felt that strong Aggregate Demand growth was infla-tionary; the policy would *counter* that tendency and "cool" the economy down. The contractionary effects of the policy, if successful, are shown in **Figures 1** and **2** under the assumption that the economy begins at a point of expansion where AD=AS above potential GDP and prices are "high."

The increase in the required reserve ratio causes a leftward shift in the Aggregate Demand curve followed by the usual adjustments: rising inventories, falling prices, reduced output and employment, and, as wages fall, a return to long-run equilibrium.

15.1.2 Decreasing the Required Reserve Ratio

Reducing the required reserve ratio will encourage banks to lend more. However, there is no guarantee that they will do so! Banks may choose to hold more in reserve than is required, so that a policy of reducing the required reserve ratio may have no effect on the economy at all!

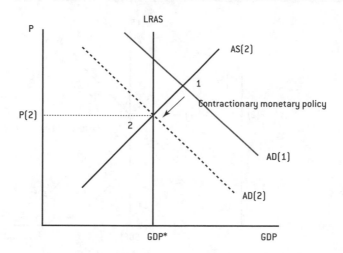

If however the policy does encourage more bank lending, then the impact on the economy is exactly symmetric to the case in **Section 15.1.1**: Increased bank lending may reduce world interest rates by making loans less scarce, causing Consumption and Investment spending rise. That increase in lending is world-wide (because the market for loans is an international market), and so the increased lending to foreigners causes U.S. banks to increase their demand for foreign currency, which causes foreign currency prices to rise and the value of the dollar to fall: the rise in the U.S. trade balance provides further stimulus of U.S. Aggregate Demand. (Note that an alternative explanation is that U.S. rates of return temporarily seem less attractive to foreigners and demand for dollars falls, causing the dollar to depreciate; either explanation is acceptable.)

FIGURE 2:

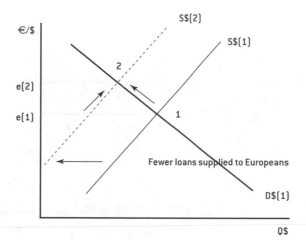

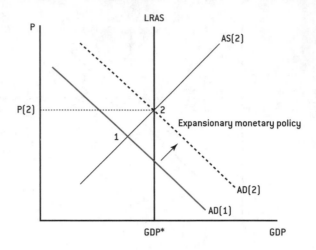

This policy might be chosen if the Fed wanted to *counter* what it believed was a recessionary decline in U.S. Aggregate Demand. The expansionary effects of the policy, if successful, are shown in **Figures 3** and **4** under the assumption that the economy begins at a point of recession where AD=AS below potential GDP.

In the long run, the *expansionary monetary policy* has no impact on real wages, employment, or GDP, but prices are higher (more inflation) and the dollar depreciates.

FIGURE 4:

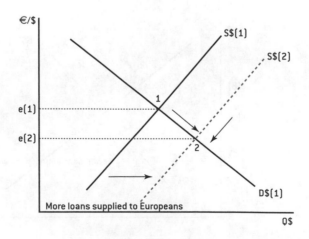

15.2 A SECOND FED POLICY OPTION: CHANGING THE DISCOUNT RATE

The discount rate is the noncompetitive interest rate charged by the Fed in its capacity as lender of last resort; it is the rate banks pay if they borrow from the regional Federal Reserve Bank. They may only borrow at this discount rate if they have fallen below the required reserve ratio.

15.2.1 Raising the Discount Rate

The higher the discount rate, the more nervous banks become about running low on reserves and they reduce lending in order to avoid the risk of having to pay a high borrowing cost. The impact on Aggregate Demand, prices, and the value of the U.S. currency is exactly the same as in the contractionary monetary policy example outlined in **Section 15.1.1**.

15.2.2 Reducing the Discount Rate

The lower the discount rate, the less banks care about running short of reserves and so they *may* increase their lending in order to earn interest income. On the other hand, they may not! Banks may have their own reasons for thinking the investment climate extremely risky, and a lower discount rate may not be enough to encourage them to lend more.

If a reduction in the discount rate does have the effect of stimulating bank lending, then the impact of the policy on Aggregate Demand, prices, and the value of the U.S. currency is exactly the same as in the expansionary monetary policy example shown in **Figures 3** and **4**.

15.3 FED POLICY OPTION: CHANGING THE TARGET FEDERAL FUNDS RATE

Should banks run below the required level of reserves, they face paying the discount rate exogenously set by the Fed if they choose to borrow from that institution; they might alternatively borrow from another bank in the (interbank) federal funds market. The third policy tool used by the Fed Reserve is used to affect the interest rate charged in that competitive market, known as the *federal funds rate*.

The FOMC knows that the fewer reserves banks have, the less likely they are to lend. Thus, the more scarce reserves are, the higher interest rates should be in general and in the federal funds market in particular. Symmetrically, the more reserves banks have, the less scarce loans will be and so the lower interest rates will be in all markets, including the federal funds market.

The Fed will *target* (aim for) a federal funds rate that reflects the amount of lending they'd like to have banks do. The Fed affects the federal funds rate by changing the number of reserves banks have, and then letting the market do the rest. The Fed changes bank reserves through *open market operations*.

15.3.1 Contractionary Open Market Operations: Raising the Target Federal Funds Rate

The regional U.S. Federal Reserve Banks are privately-run institutions that make loans and hold assets, much like regular banks. Unlike other banks, Federal Reserve Bank assets *must* include government securities. Open Market Operations involve the sale or purchase of government securities on the "open market" by the regional Federal Reserve Banks.

An individual that wants to put his or her savings into a government security will pay the market price for that asset; if that individual buys the security from another individual, then there is a transfer of deposit money from one account to another, but no change in M2 and no change in the amount of reserves banks hold.

If however an individual buys a government security from a regional Fed, then when the Fed cashes the check *the money leaves the banking system*: there are now fewer reserves in the banking system. Fewer loans will be made, and interest rates will rise because of the increase in loan scarcity. The FOMC will continue to order its regional banks to sell securities on the open market until loan scarcity results in a federal funds rate equal to the target.

Of course, other interest rates will rise as well because banks will reduce lending in other markets too, driving up other interest rates. Thus contractionary monetary policy will affect Investment, Consumption, and exchange rates in the same way as do the other contractionary policies described in **Sections 15.1** and **15.2**.

15.3.2 Expansionary Open Market Operations: Lowering the Target Federal Funds Rate

In an expansionary Open Market Operation, the FOMC orders the regional Federal Reserve Banks to purchase government securities from private individuals that wish to sell them. The regional Feds are profit-making institutions—they try to get the security for the lowest price they can, but they will offer whatever price is necessary in order to encourage holders of government debt to sell. To keep holders of securities from trying to get an especially good price out of such a rich customer as a regional Federal Reserve Bank, Fed open market operations are always conducted anonymously through reliable financial market traders.

If the regional Fed purchases a security from a private individual, then when that individual cashes the check there is a transfer of money from the Fed to a private banking account and *money enters the banking system*: there are now more reserves in the banking system. Banks that hold more reserves may choose to lend more and, if they do, reduced loan scarcity will drive down interest rates in many markets, including the federal funds market. The FOMC will continue to order its regional banks to purchase securities until loan scarcity results in a federal funds rate equal to the target.

Because lending may become less scarce in other markets as well as in the federal funds market, the expansionary monetary policy may affect Investment, Consumption, and exchange rates in exactly the same way as the expansionary policies that were described in **Sections 15.1** and **15.2**. On the other hand, banks may *only* be willing to increase lending in the relatively low-risk interbank market and *not* in the consumer debt or capital markets, in which case the open market operation may have little or no impact on Consumption or Investment in Aggregate Demand.

15.4.1 Contractionary Monetary Policy Is More Effective Than Expansionary Monetary Policy

Short-run monetary policy goals are usually concerned with countering perceived Aggregate Demand shocks: The goal is to reduce unemployment during recessions and to reduce inflationary pressures during booms. It turns out that it is much easier to do the latter—to counter a boom—than it is to stimulate short-run Aggregate Demand. The reason is that the monetary authority can always force banks to reduce lending; if it cannot discourage lending by raising banks' borrowing costs (through a higher discount rate or higher federal funds rate), then the Fed can simply resort to the brute force method of raising the required reserve ratio. If banks must hold more in reserve, then lending to households and firms will decrease, reducing Aggregate Demand. In practice, the U.S. Fed has not needed to resort to this brute force method and instead has always simply raised the discount rate and target federal funds rate together in order to provide banks the incentive to temporarily reduce their lending.

Economists sometimes liken the economic impact of contractionary monetary policy to *pulling on a string*; if you imagine tying a string around Aggregate Expenditures, you can always pull back on the string and pull Aggregate Demand along as well.

By the same analogy, however, if you keep that string tied around Aggregate Demand and try to *push* on it (to push AD outward), the string will move but nothing will happen to AD—the string just bunches up and AD goes nowhere. ***Critics of the effectiveness of expansionary monetary policy liken it to pushing on a string***, arguing that it has no impact on real spending.

15.4.2 Why Expansionary Monetary Policy May Be Like "Pushing on a String"

Unlike fiscal policy, there are no offsetting influences on Aggregate Demand as a result of expansionary monetary policy: Expansionary monetary policy doesn't *cost* anything to the government as it is just an exchange of assets by the regional Feds (cash and deposits held by the regional Feds are exchanged for government securities). Moreover, the impact of an expansionary monetary policy on the exchange rate is to cause it to depreciate, which only further stimulates Aggregate Demand. In other words, all of the endogenous expenditure categories of Aggregate Demand (Consumption, Investment, and the Trade Balance) move in the same direction if they move at all as a result of monetary policy.

So what's the problem with expansionary monetary policy? Why might it sometimes be like pushing on a string? The problem is that monetary policy has a permanent effect on inflation, and that effect is something that may be well understood by both lenders and workers. Their expectations about inflation may undo the effectiveness of counter-cyclical monetary policy.

15.4.2.1 Expansionary Monetary Policy and Expected Inflation: Capital Markets
Any of the three expansionary monetary policy tools available to the Fed reduce the expected costs of making loans by reducing the penalty for having fewer reserves (either by reducing the required reserve ratio or by lowering the banks' costs of borrowing). Assuming that monetary

policy does not affect potential GDP, more loans means more demand for goods and services and higher prices. Thus while one cost of making loans is falling as a result of policy, another cost (inflation) is rising; inflation, you remember, is costly to lenders because it eats away at the purchasing power of the contracted repayment amount.

If inflation is expected to increase, banks will demand a higher nominal interest rate on long-term lending in order to cover their costs. Thus the nominal interest rate charged on *overnight* loans, like the federal funds rate, may *fall* at the same time that *long term* nominal interest rates, like the rates charged on capital goods, mortgages, car loans, and so on, *rise*. The net effect on the expected real return from making a long-term loan may be unchanged (higher nominal rate to cover higher expected inflation), so there may be no impact at all of the policy on lending to households or firms and therefore no change in the Consumption or Investment components of AD. (Note that this implies that the capital account, in real terms, is also unchanged, so that there is also no change in real spending on the trade balance.)

The effectiveness of expansionary monetary policy will then depend in part on how accurate banks' expectations are about the inflationary impact of the policy. Banks may be very rational but still make mistakes about how quickly the policy will affect prices, how quickly exchange rates will adjust to their Purchasing Power Parity position, and so on.

15.4.2.2 Expansionary Monetary Policy and Expected Inflation: Labor Markets

Recessions only persist in our model economy if labor markets fail to adjust to their long-run equilibrium or, in other words, if real wages will not fall to their long-run levels. Once real wages begin to fall, employment and GDP increase and the recession ends. It may take some time for workers to negotiate or accept lower nominal wage contracts and so recessions may not quickly resolve.

One of the ways that expansionary monetary policy works is by causing prices to rise—pushing down the real wage. This is an advantage to unemployed workers, as the lower real wages allow perfectly competitive firms to increase employment (at lower marginal productivity of labor) and still cover their costs. It is however a disadvantage to *employed* workers, who are actually better off during the recession because of the higher real wage earned.

If employed workers accurately forecast the inflationary impact of an expansionary monetary policy, they will want higher nominal wages. If they are able to block competitive pressures from unemployed workers (say, by unionizing) then nominal wages may rise as prices rise, resulting in no change in the real wage and consequently no change in employment or GDP! (And, of course, if workers and employers overestimate inflation and negotiate too high a wage, then the recession will get worse!)

The effect of expansionary monetary policy on labor markets depends, generally, both on the accuracy of worker/firm inflationary expectations as well as on the relative power of working versus unemployed members of the workforce in determining wages. In a perfectly competitive market, unemployed workers will keep nominal wages from begin driven up during downturns. However, if unemployed workers are barred from competing in the wage process either because of unionization or some other barrier to entry (such as skill acquisition), then monetary policy may be purely inflationary.

15.5 CONSTRAINTS ON THE EFFECTIVENESS OF LONG-TERM MONETARY POLICIES

The long-term goal of monetary policy is that of price level stability. Long-term policy goals by the Fed therefore refer to inflationary or deflationary "pressures" on the economy. So long as wages and nominal interest rates rise at the same rate as do prices, it doesn't matter what the long-run inflation level is. What the Fed tries to do is to keep annual inflation rates fairly constant at a low level so that there are no surprises that might cause either boom or recession.

Why not target an inflation rate of zero? One answer is that the Fed worries that if annual interest rates get too close to zero, that an unexpected fall in MFP could make the equilibrium nominal interest rate a negative number! There's nothing wrong with that in theory, but in the real world banking institutions don't contract for negative interest rates.

One long-run relationship between money growth and prices is defined by the Quantity Theory of Money. Writing that equation in growth rates, we have the following relationship:

$$\dot{M} + \dot{V} = \dot{P} + \dot{GDP}$$

where M is the money supply (M2, for example) and V is the Velocity (of M2).

Assuming V is constant (i.e. there are no technological changes that affect velocity), this can be rewritten as:

$$\dot{M} - \dot{GDP} = \dot{P}$$

The Fed achieves its inflationary target by setting money growth at a certain pace relative to expected GDP growth. Because the Fed cannot affect GDP growth (we assume!), they must first forecast GDP growth before setting monetary policy. In other words, in order to set long-term monetary policy, they need to forecast MFP growth (as well as population growth, of course).

Forecasting MFP is not trivial! It is not even clear that we do a particularly good job at measuring *current* MFP; constructing a forecast of future data based on shoddy current data is particularly difficult.

The model we are using in this text assumes that technological progress is exogenous, which means that we cannot model or forecast its progress based on observations in any market. The Fed, on the other hand, devotes a great many resources to trying to model technological progress and to trying to improve upon MFP measurement, and bankers and labor union economists and a myriad of other economic analysts are busy at the same thing because they will all be affected by the inflation that will result if the Fed is wrong about its long-run MFP (GDP) forecast.

15.6 CONSTRAINTS ON MONETARY POLICY IN SMALL COUNTRIES

Monetary policy only affects lending to households and firms if it also affects the equilibrium cost of borrowing; in an economy open to international capital inflows, that means that the change in domestic bank behavior must be large enough to affect world loan scarcity. Small countries that would otherwise be unable to affect world interest rates will sometimes impose *international capital controls*, or legal restrictions on financial flows of money across their borders: Some borrowing from or lending to foreigners may be legally permissible but there may be taxes or quotas (limits) on the amount of the capital flow. Capital controls reduce the level of the capital stock and so are frowned on by international economists, but they give monetary authorities in small countries more control over domestic Aggregate Demand.

Small countries without capital controls may be unable to significantly affect Consumption and Investment spending through monetary policy, but they can still affect their trade balance. Moreover, trade is usually a large share of Aggregate Demand in small economies, so this aspect of monetary policymaking is still a powerful tool. Rather than target an interest rate with monetary policy, these countries may instead target an exchange rate: this is known as a *fixed (or pegged) exchange rate* system. Countries like the U.S. that target the interest rate operate in a *flexible exchange rate* system.

In other words, monetary policymakers have a choice about which price they want to target: they can choose either one particular interest rate (in the U.S., we choose to target the federal funds rate) or one particular exchange rate (countries usually choose to target their exchange rate with the U.S., Japan, or the European Union). In that case the policy will exactly like an exchange rate policy.

Figures 5 and **6** depict an economy that has a fixed exchange rate with respect to the U.S. dollar. The economy is in recession: AD has fallen, driving up inventories and encouraging firms to cut back on employment, resulting in lower prices (the remaining workers are more efficient due to diminishing returns to labor in production) and lower output. The monetary authority in a pegged exchange-rate system may choose to target a lower fixed exchange rate; this will make their exports seem cheaper to the U.S. (X increases) and at the same time make foreign products will seem more expensive to domestic consumers (M falls).

The monetary authority may achieve this through expansionary open market operations that stimulate increased bank lending to foreigners and therefore increased demand for dollars (increased supply of Pesos in the Peso-per-Dollar exchange market), or their treasury or central

FIGURE 5:

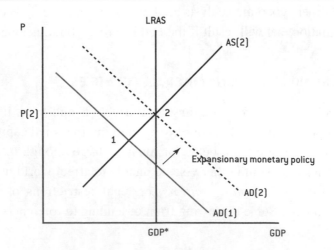

AN INTRODUCTION TO MACROECONOMICS

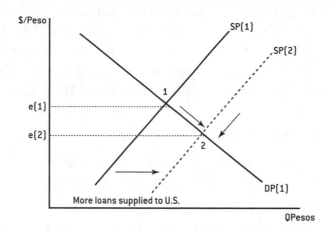

bank may buy U.S. assets directly rather than work through their domestic banking system. S>D for Pesos and the currency depreciates. X rises and M falls, shifting AD to the right and bringing the economy out of recession.

PRACTICE PROBLEMS

1. Explain in detail how the Fed goes about achieving a higher target federal funds rate.

2. Explain in words why it is that a contractionary monetary policy like the one in Question 1 might cause an appreciation of the dollar.

3. Going through each component of Aggregate Demand, explain the likely total impact of a contractionary monetary policy on AD.

SUGGESTED ANSWERS

1. The FOMC orders the regional Federal Reserve Banks to sell government securities. When private households or institutions buy these securities on the open market, the money used to pay for them leaves the private banking system and leaves M2. Bank reserves fall outside of Federal Reserve Banks. These private banks need to get their reserves back up to cover the required reserve ratio, and so reduce their lending. As loans become more scarce, interest rates rise. One of the rates that rises in the interbank lending rate (the federal funds rate). The FOMC continues to order the sale (or purchase) of securities as needed to keep the ffr at its target level.

2. If banks reduce their lending, they also reduce the amount of international lending they are making. That means that the banks' demand for foreign assets is falling, and so private bank demand for foreign currency (needed to buy those assets) is also falling. Reduced demand for foreign currency makes their currency fall in price (dollars per foreign currency unit falls), which implies that our currency is rising in price relative to theirs (Foreign currency units per dollar rises). The dollar appreciates.

3. Consider each AE component of Aggregate Demand to see that AD unambiguously falls:

C: If lending decreases and we are large enough to affect world real interest rates, then rates will rise. Higher real rates means more Savings and therefore less Consumption.

Planned I: If world real rates rise, then firms need a higher mpk to cover costs and they reduce I. The marginal productivity of capital rises (diminishing returns) until mpk=r (perfect competition), so that means I falls until mpk=r.

G is exogenous and unchanged.

X-M: The dollar appreciates, which makes our exports seem more expensive to foreigners and X falls. M rises because foreign currency and foreign goods seem cheaper. X-M falls.

THINGS TO DO WITH MACROECONOMICS

At this point you may be feeling a bit overwhelmed! The advantage of having been exposed to so much, however, is that you can now *do* so much with your understanding of the economy. You now have to tools to help you to understand basic questions about what to do with your savings, how much to save, which economic policies you support, and so on.

The following sections include some of the types of questions even non-economists will want to be able to address, and which you are now capable of thinking about in a logical way.

16.1   IS THIS A GOOD TIME TO BUY STOCKS?

Fewer than half of U.S. households own stocks (either directly or indirectly through a pension plan), but with luck you'll end up being in the half that does! If so, you'll be constantly faced with the question of whether it is currently a good time to buy or sell these financial assets that will be contributing to your overall wealth and to your retirement plans.

You know from this course what a stock is (part-ownership of a firm) and what determines its value (expected future MFP, inflation, and market bubbles). You also know that before buying a stock you should also consider the expected returns from *other* financial assets (corporate or government bonds, bank deposits, or investment in your own home) because you want to put your money where it will earn the highest expected return. In equilibrium, of course, all expected real rates of return are the same, but you'd like to be one of the profit-makers that drive all returns to equality!

Moreover, you know that if you buy a foreign stock, that you'll be concerned about the expected exchange rate in the period when you will sell. And you also know that if you buy a domestic stock, that *its* value may fluctuate with the value of the U.S. exchange rate because of the influence of foreign savers on U.S. asset prices, and so that'll be a consideration for you as well..

And finally, you know that the future value of your stock will be affected by how much demand there is for stocks relative to other financial assets, which means that you'll be concerned about the way that interest rates are affected both by monetary and fiscal policy. So, you'll want to do a rough forecast of the implications of current trends in the U.S. government budget deficit on real interest rates, and of the implications of current trends in U.S. monetary policy on both interest rates and inflation rates.

Now, this may all make buying stocks seem even more intimidating than it did before you took the course! But really, there is not so much to all of this—the information is easy to get. Headlines will read "The Fed is cracking down on inflation", for example, and you'll know that this means that old bonds will be worth more (higher real return if inflation falls) and stocks likely worth less (by arbitrage). Or you might see a headline about mass layoffs at a major U.S. firm that makes you concerned about trend changes in MFP in all industries. And because you have a background in the vocabulary and theory of how markets work, you'll be able to read the business section of the paper that can help synthesize all of these things for you if you don't want to take the time yourself.

16.2   IS THE LARGE U.S. GOVERNMENT BUDGET DEFICIT BAD FOR THE ECONOMY?

This question resurrects itself during every cyclical downturn, as falling tax revenues, often coupled with out-and-out tax cuts, cause the budget deficit to increase right at a time when the economy is already in trouble. You know from this class that the answer to the question of whether deficits are harmful depends importantly on two issues: Will households save for the future debt repayment? Is the government borrowing large enough to affect world interest rates and therefore domestic Investment spending? Your opinion about those two questions will determine your opinion about whether you support or oppose an Administration plan to cut taxes, but it will also affect your view about the value of your financial assets (see **Section 16.1**).

16.3   IS A "STRONG" DOLLAR A GOOD THING?

You should immediately be able to answer this one: No! But it's not a bad thing either. Getting hung up on the idea that a "strong" or "expensive" dollar somehow reflects economic strength is a common misperception among people who haven't learnt economics. Now you have the tools to tell them so! An expensive dollar is no more good or bad than is an expensive apple— there are buyers and sellers in the aggregate market and something that is bad for the buyers is equally good for the sellers!

Now, there is an interesting question about whether *unpredicted* changes in the value of the dollar are a bad thing. If there is *uncertainty* about the future dollar value, that exchange-rate risk may deter inflows of foreign savings because of the implied uncertainty about the real return from the loans; fewer loans from foreigners means lower Investment spending here, and lower real wages and GDP in the future. In fact, you've seen that the U.S. Treasury does it's best to smooth out temporary wiggles in the exchange rate precisely because of the damage it can cause, but it doesn't try to affect the equilibrium value to make the dollar either "strong" or "weak".

Moreover, you also know that any permanent change in the value of the dollar—making it either permanently strong or weak—will eventually be reflected in a permanent change in prices in the opposite direction! Goods market arbitrage will make meaningless any relative strength or weakness of the nominal exchange rate.

16.4   SUMMARY

This textbook is titled **An Introduction to Macroeconomics** because it is precisely that: an *introduction*. It's very useful to have an introductory model of the economy that gives you a general sense of how sectors of the economy influence one another. At the same time, the model that we've seen has had to make many important assumptions in order to allow us to keep track of everything. Moreover, we've restricted our analysis to graphical representations of demand and supply in various macro markets, and those graphical representations only give us a *qualitative* sense of where things are going—we can't nail down an exact GDP forecast or even say how long it will take to get to equilibrium unless we start plugging in numbers, and in order to use those numbers we need to use some fairly sophisticated mathematics to solve the models. Some economists also spend their careers developing and using sophisticated statistical methods to see if the data line up with the predictions of the model (to try to test the models).

That means that to continue in economics, you'll eventually want to take some supporting math and statistics courses, but it's worth it! Using math we can model the frictions in labor markets that we know to be important, we can disaggregate the macro model to consider linkages between, for example, skilled and unskilled workers or traded and non-traded goods or between perfectly-competitive and monopolistically-competitive firms. Those types of questions are much too difficult to address using a two-dimensional AD-AS graph like the one from the intro course, but they are extremely interesting and important issues affecting the economy today.